JESUS, FADS, & THE MEDIA
The Passion & Popular Culture

RELIGION & MODERN CULTURE
Title List

JESUS, FADS, & THE MEDIA
The Passion & Popular Culture

by Michael Evans

Mason Crest Publishers
Philadelphia

Mason Crest Publishers Inc.
370 Reed Road
Broomall, Pennsylvania 19008
(866) MCP-BOOK (toll free)

First printing
1 2 3 4 5 6 7 8 9 10

Library of Congress Cataloging-in-Publication Data
Evans, Michael.
  Jesus, fads, & the media : the passion & popular culture / by Michael Evans.
      p. cm. — (Religion and modern culture)
  Includes bibliographical references and index.
  ISBN 1-59084-972-8 ISBN 1-59084-970-1 (series)
  1. Popular culture—Religious aspects—Christianity. 2. Mass media—Religious aspects—Christianity. I. Title: Jesus, fads, and the media. II. Title. III. Series.
  BR115.C8E935 2006
  261—dc22
                                         2005018591

Produced by Harding House Publishing Service, Inc.
www.hardinghousepages.com
Interior design by Dianne Hodack.
Cover design by MK Bassett-Harvey.
Printed in India.

CONTENTS

INTRODUCTION

by Dr. Marcus J. Borg

You are about to begin an important and exciting experience: the study of modern religion. Knowing about religion—and religions—is vital for understanding our neighbors, whether they live down the street or across the globe.

Despite the modern trend toward religious doubt, most of the world's population continues to be religious. Of the approximately six billion people alive today, around two billion are Christians, one billion are Muslims, 800 million are Hindus, and 400 million are Buddhists. Smaller numbers are Sikhs, Shinto, Confucian, Taoist, Jewish, and indigenous religions.

Religion plays an especially important role in North America. The United States is the most religious country in the Western world: about 80 percent of Americans say that religion is "important" or "very important" to them. Around 95 percent say they believe in God. These figures are very different in Europe, where the percentages are much smaller. Canada is "in between": the figures are lower than for the United States, but significantly higher than in Europe. In Canada, 68 percent of citizens say religion is of "high importance," and 81 percent believe in God or a higher being.

The United States is largely Christian. Around 80 percent describe themselves as Christian. In Canada, professing Christians are 77 percent of the population. But religious diversity is growing. According to Harvard scholar Diana Eck's recent book *A New Religious America*, the United States has recently become the most religiously diverse country in the world. Canada is also a country of great religious variety.

Fifty years ago, religious diversity in the United States meant Protestants, Catholics, and Jews, but since the 1960s, immigration from Asia, the Middle East, and Africa has dramatically increased the number of people practicing other religions. There are now about six million Muslims, four million Buddhists, and a million Hindus in the United States. To compare these figures to two historically important Protestant denominations in the United States, about 3.5 million are Presbyterians and 2.5 million are Episcopalians. There are more Buddhists in the United States than either of these denominations, and as many Muslims as the two denominations combined. This means that knowing about other religions is not just knowing about people in other parts of the world—but about knowing people in our schools, workplaces, and neighborhoods.

Moreover, religious diversity does not simply exist between religions. It is found within Christianity itself:

• There are many different forms of Christian worship. They range from Quaker silence to contemporary worship with rock music to traditional liturgical worship among Catholics and Episcopalians to Pentecostal enthusiasm and speaking in tongues.

- Christians are divided about the importance of an afterlife. For some, the next life—a paradise beyond death—is their primary motive for being Christian. For other Christians, the afterlife does not matter nearly as much. Instead, a relationship with God that transforms our lives this side of death is the primary motive.
- Christians are divided about the Bible. Some are biblical literalists who believe that the Bible is to be interpreted literally and factually as the inerrant revelation of God, true in every respect and true for all time. Other Christians understand the Bible more symbolically as the witness of two ancient communities—biblical Israel and early Christianity—to their life with God.

Christians are also divided about the role of religion in public life. Some understand "separation of church and state" to mean "separation of religion and politics." Other Christians seek to bring Christian values into public life. Some (commonly called "the Christian Right") are concerned with public policy issues such as abortion, prayer in schools, marriage as only heterosexual, and pornography. Still other Christians name the central public policy issues as American imperialism, war, economic injustice, racism, health care, and so forth. For the first group, values are primarily concerned with individual behavior. For the second group, values are also concerned with group behavior and social systems. The study of religion in North America involves not only becoming aware of other religions but also becoming aware of differences within Christianity itself. Such study can help us to understand people with different convictions and practices.

And there is one more reason why such study is important and exciting: religions deal with the largest questions of life. These questions are intellectual, moral, and personal. Most centrally, they are:

- What is real? The religions of the world agree that "the real" is more than the space-time world of matter and energy.
- How then shall we live?
- How can we be "in touch" with "the real"? How can we connect with it and become more deeply centered in it?

This series will put you in touch with other ways of seeing reality and how to live.

Chapter 1

THE PASSION OF CHRIST

RELIGION & MODERN CULTURE

When you hear the word "passion," you probably think of steamy romance novels and R-rated movies. In today's conversation, we usually use the word in connection with extreme sexual emotion. It's possible you might connect "passion" with something you care about a great deal, something that truly excites you on an intellectual and emotional level—as in, "Sports are my passion," or "I'm passionate about social justice." In either usage of the word, it's probably difficult to see how this word connects to Jesus of Nazareth, the historical person who stands at the center of Christianity.

The original meaning of the word "passion," however, came from Latin words that meant "suffering, enduring"; in fact, "passion" comes from the same roots as the word "patient." Through centuries of Christian tradition, this word came to be connected to the physical, emotional, and spiritual pain Christ experienced when he was executed by being hung from a cross.

Whatever our religious backgrounds, almost all of us are familiar with the image of Christ dying on a cross. The picture has been portrayed again and again, from famous artwork to jewelry, from cemeteries to tattoos. This image has infiltrated our culture's collective imagination; whatever our beliefs, the cross is a part of the vocabulary we all have available to us when we think about life.

Over the years, however, the cross has become so familiar that it is often merely decorative. While Catholic Christians continued to portray Christ's body on the cross, Protestant Christians removed him, as though it would be poor taste to have a dying man hanging at the front of a church or around one's neck. (When you think about it, of course, it is a little strange: imagine if Christ had been executed by hanging or in an electric chair—would people then wear tiny gold nooses or place artistic electric chairs at the front of their worship buildings?) In any case, when something becomes familiar, it often loses some of its power to influence human emotion and thought. Despite the countless works of art inspired by Christ's life and death, these images had become, in effect, passionless—devoid of emotion and energy.

Director Mel Gibson wanted to change that. He wanted people to re-experience—in an intense and emotional way—the Passion of Christ. The Passion, Gibson believed, could be made relevant for modern culture.

GLOSSARY

anti-Semitism: Hostility toward or discrimination against Jews as a relgious or ethnic group.

Augustinian: A religious group of nuns or monks that consider themselves to be disciples of Augustine, the fourth-century Christian saint.

paradoxically: Appearing to be contradictory.

pilgrimages: Spiritual journeys to shrines or sacred places.

sadistic: Having to do with an unnatural delight or pleasure derived from the pain of others.

secular: Relating to worldly rather than religious concerns.

Western: Having to do with the cultures of Europe and North America, which are based in the traditions and philosophies of the Greeks and Romans.

MEL GIBSON'S GOSPEL: "THE PASSION OF THE CHRIST"

One night in the Garden of Gethsemane, a man named Jesus bent low among the trees on his knees, praying desperately. A dark, cloaked figure whispered in his ear, trying to distract the man from his prayer.

"Do you really believe that one man can bear the full burden of sin?" said the human-like Satan in a voice that was neither male nor female. "No one man can carry this burden, I tell you. It's too heavy. No one can save their souls. No one. Ever."

However, Jesus continued to pray. All but one of his twelve disciples slept nearby, even though he had asked for their help in praying. They were his friends; why wouldn't they join him in this hour? Jesus was desperate, yet focused. He did not want to do it, but he was obeying his Father, the one to whom he prayed.

The genderless Satan tried another temptation: "Who is your father? Who are you?"

Jesus did not answer. He saw a snake slither from Satan's cloak. As it approached him, he stood and stomped on it.

Satan disappeared and quickly reappeared elsewhere: with Judas, one of Jesus's friends. This time Satan took the form of a terrifying ghoul, flashing before Judas's eyes. Judas, the betrayer, cowered like a frightened little child and then ran off to do what he had planned.

Hours later, Judas arrived in the garden with a mob of temple guards carrying weapons. Noise and confusion awakened the other eleven disciples. Judas greeted Jesus with a friendly kiss on the cheek, indicating whom they should arrest.

As guards led Jesus from place to place, religious leaders accused him, Roman government officials questioned him, and soldiers mocked him. Authorities ordered his execution. Jesus was to be nailed onto a cross made of wood and humiliated until he finally bled to death or suffocated under the weight of his own body.

Before his execution, soldiers brought Jesus to a courtyard, where they tied him to a post and beat him with sticks and a whip. During the beatings, Jesus looked up to see his mother, Mary, looking on with tears in her eyes. His right eye was swollen shut from the bruising as they struck him on the head with sticks. His obedience contrasted with his winces that coincided with the sound of stick hitting flesh. His body was cut and bloody, yet the soldiers, with cruel and hungry looks in their

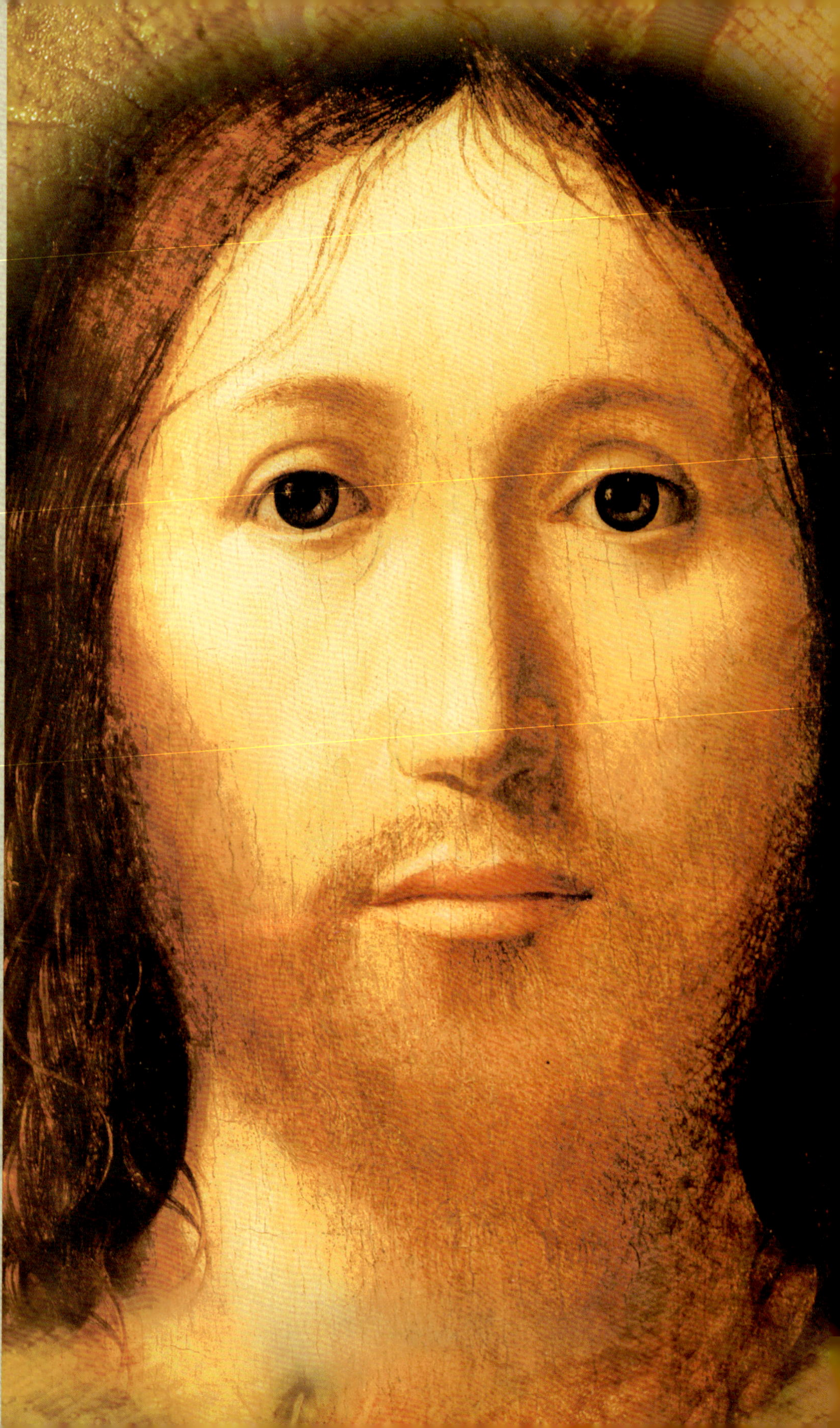

CHANGING IMAGES OF CHRIST

Artists in different eras have chosen to portray Jesus in different ways. Gretchen Passantino claims that Gibson's Jesus is more realistic than previous portrayals of Christ:

> Gone is the effeminate Aryan proverb-spouting Jesus of the 1950s. Gone is the virile anti-hero Jesus of the 1960s. Gone is the mentally ill and emotionally conflicted superstar Jesus of the 1970s. Gone is the sexually motivated revolutionary Jesus of the last part of the century. In the Jesus of *The Passion of the Christ* we encounter the Jesus of scripture: God manifest in the flesh, fully human and fully God, totally committed to his redemptive work on behalf of a humanity that scorned him, empowered by the Holy Spirit to endure unspeakable torture and pain. . . . In this Jesus we see the power in suffering, the grace in enduring, the mercy in sacrifice, the strength in submission.

It could be that the needs of each time period dictate a different spiritual hunger that leads to varying expressions of Christ's nature. People in the future may come to realize that Mel Gibson's version of the Jesus story also reflected the specific needs of its time.

"Don't you realize that I am able right now to call to my Father, and twelve companies . . . of fighting angels would be here, battle ready? But if I did that, how would the Scriptures come true that say this is the way it has to be?"

—*Jesus, according to the Gospel of Matthew, in* The Message

eyes, continued to beat him. Jesus looked up again to see Satan, pleased at his suffering, holding a demon child with a sickly smile. Jesus fell; the soldiers whipped him while the crowd watched. Small pieces of flesh were torn from his body, and his agony shone through his open left eye. Yet they continued to beat him. He lay in a large pool of his own blood, and they beat him again until, mercifully, the soldiers were stopped.

Mel Gibson portrayed this scene in the film *The Passion of the Christ*, which he produced and directed in 2004. The film's story is about the final twelve hours of Jesus's life. Gibson, who is a devout Roman Catholic Christian, wanted to create a film that would give viewers a deep emotional experience. He felt that by making the film he was completing his mission from God, and so he spent more than $20 million of his own money to ensure his vision was completed.

The Passion of the Christ was so popular that it became one of the top-ten selling films of all time. Opening-weekend viewers lined up at theaters around the country, sometimes with church groups. On the Internet, television, and in publications, the media reported countless strong viewer reactions to the film.

"This is my version of what happened, according to the Gospels, and what I wanted to show."

—Mel Gibson

THE PASSION STORY OVER THE CENTURIES

This type of connection between Gibson's religious beliefs and popular culture is nothing new. Although *Western* thinking often draws a line between the *secular* world and the sacred, in reality, religion and culture have always interacted; it is impossible to separate one from the other. Our culture affects how we think about religion—and religion shapes our culture. As a result, it's only to be expected that over the centuries, the story of Jesus's Passion would be retold again and again, in popular plays, paintings, and songs.

While retelling the Passion story, different filmmakers, preachers, artists, and storytellers make choices about what to add, take away, or emphasize. The most common version of the Passion story comes from a mix of the four Gospels. These are books in the New Testament of the Christian Bible written after Jesus's death by four eyewitnesses. According to church tradition, they are named after their four authors: Matthew, Mark, Luke, and John. The basic plot of the Passion varies slightly between the books. Often, the Passion drama portrayed by popular culture comes from a blending of these four different points of view.

For most Christians, the Passion tells the story of the most important event in human history. It shows the character of Jesus: obedient to God, even when it came to death, willing to endure pain out of love for humanity. Christians believe that Jesus offers love and eternal life to everyone in the world. Believers have faith that Jesus has risen from the dead, is now living in heaven with his Father, and will someday return at the end of time. They often refer to Jesus as *the Christ*, Greek for "anointed one," which is similar to the Hebrew word for *Messiah*.

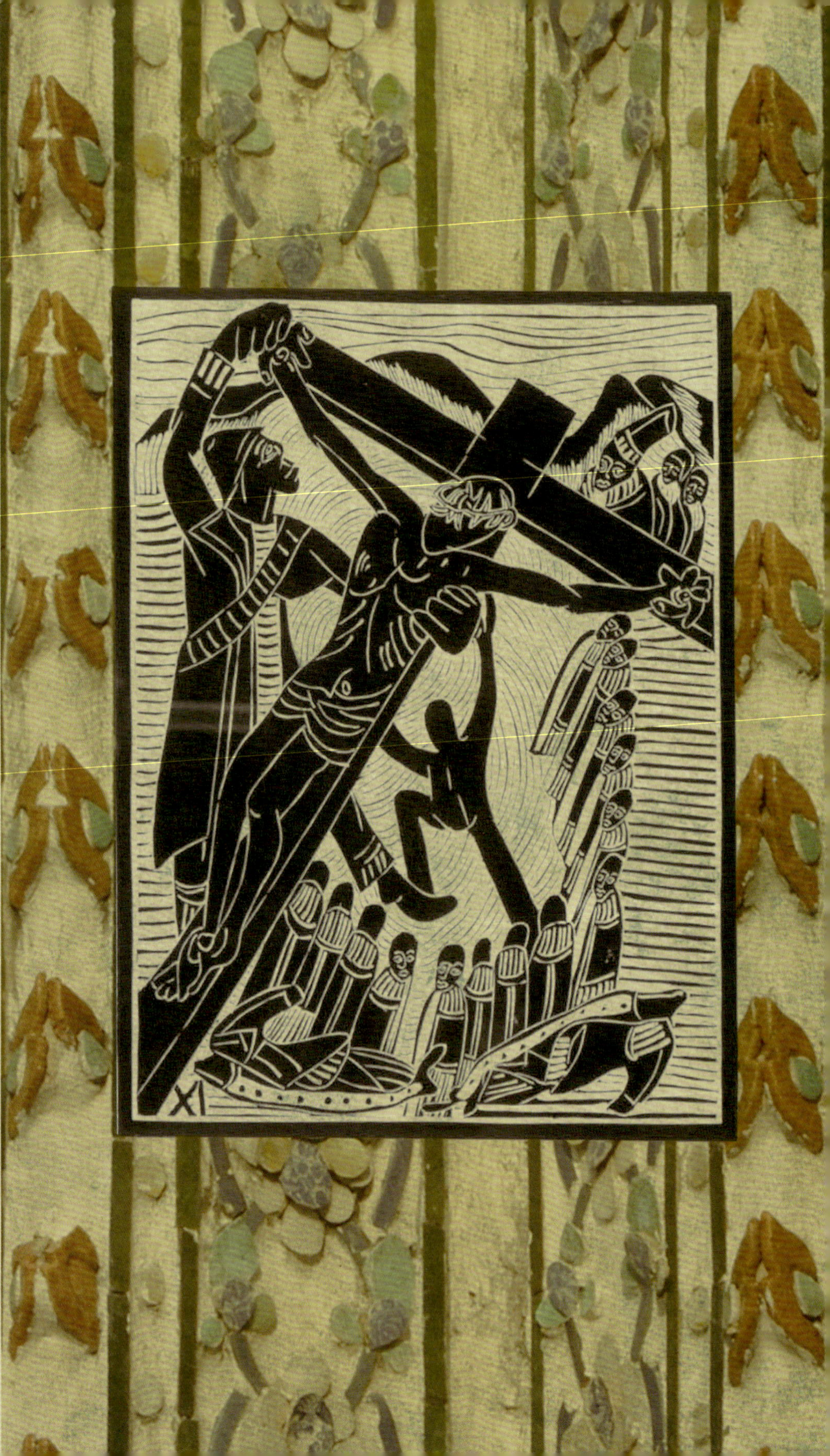
XI

THE FOURTEEN STATIONS OF THE CROSS

Station one is where Jesus is sentenced to die in
    Pilate's hall of judgment.
Station two is where Jesus is given his cross to
    carry.
Station three is where Jesus falls down for the first
    time.
Station four is where Jesus encounters his mother.
Station five is where Simon is forced to help Jesus
    carry his cross.
Station six is where Veronica wipes Jesus's face.
Station seven is where Jesus falls the second time.
Station eight is where Jesus meets the women of
    Jerusalem.
Station nine is where Jesus falls the third time.
Station ten is where Jesus is stripped of his
    garments.
Station eleven is where Jesus is nailed to the
    cross.
Station twelve is where Jesus dies.
Station thirteen is where Jesus's body is removed
    from the cross.
Station fourteen is the tomb where Jesus is laid.

RELIGION & MODERN CULTURE

In his version of Christ's story, Gibson borrowed ideas from past Passion retellings. He wanted to be creative with the plot and the characters, but he insists he did not want to stray from scripture, history, and Christian faith. He based his script on the Gospels, famous paintings, the fourteen Stations of the Cross, and *The Dolorous Gospel of Our Lord Jesus Christ*, a book of the mediations of Anne Catherine Emmerich, an ***Augustinian*** nun.

Gibson consulted respected religious leaders and scholars from Protestant, Catholic, and Jewish traditions. He wanted Christians and non-Christians to have an experience of Jesus Christ in the movie theater. At the same time, Gibson wanted to be faithful to Catholic traditions.

The fourteen Stations of the Cross (sometimes called the *Via Dolorosa*—the path of sorrow) are part of the Catholic tradition of the Passion. Each station is a piece of art representing the places Jesus went during the last hours of his life. People of faith go from station to station praying and meditating on the purpose of each one. This tradition began centuries ago when Christians were making ***pilgrimages*** to Jerusalem to see where Jesus spent his final hours. Later, these sites in Jerusalem became "stations." Since everyone could not travel to Jerusalem, the fourteen stations were re-created on the walls of Catholic churches all over Europe. Today these stations can be found on church lawns or inside buildings.

Much of Gibson's film focuses on Christ's suffering. The script was influenced by the meditations of Anne Catherine Emmerich, whose life was filled with poverty, sickness, and suffering in nineteenth-century Germany. Perhaps her own experiences influenced her perception of Christ. In any case, her visions of Jesus's flogging were graphic. By contrast, the Bible only briefly mentions his beatings, with almost no details. Emmerich's influence made Gibson's film different from past Jesus

THE PASSION AS A SPIRITUAL TOOL: A HISTORICAL PERSPECTIVE

Mel Gibson wasn't the first to dramatize the Passion of Christ as a powerful spiritual tool. During the Middle Ages, town guilds in England staged elaborate plays on outdoor wagons during the Feast of Corpus Christi (Christ's Body). The centerpiece of these plays was Jesus's death, which was portrayed as graphically and brutally as Gibson did centuries later. Nor was drama the only art form to focus on Christ's death. Medieval sermons, paintings, and spiritual practices all stressed the importance of Jesus's suffering. A medieval devotional guide titled *Meditations on the Life of Christ* told readers: "You must direct your attention to these scenes of the Passion, as if you were actually present at the Cross, and watch the Crucifixion of our Lord with affection, diligence, love, and perseverance." These words might also be used to summarize Mel Gibson's goal for his movie.

plays and films. The story's climax has usually focused on Jesus's cruci-fixion, which is described in more detail in the Bible, but in *The Passion of the Christ*, Jesus's beating is the climax, lasting on screen for seem-ingly endless minutes. Gibson said he was attempting to visually re-create the agony Christ suffered on behalf of humanity. Many viewers disagreed; instead, they felt the long scene was needlessly violent, a near-***sadistic*** glorification of human agony.

DOES THE PASSION PROMOTE HATRED & VIOLENCE?

The Passion is a controversial movie. Some of the most serious criticism came from Jewish leaders, who complained that the movie could encour-age hatred toward Jews. Over many centuries, Christians have accused, fought, and killed Jewish people for allegedly executing Jesus. Interpretations of the Bible have worsened such ***anti-Semitism***. In Matthew's Gospel, the crowd demanded that Pilate crucify Jesus saying, "Let his blood be on us and on our children!" Some Christians have un-derstood that statement to mean Jewish people are responsible for Jesus's death.

Gibson says he does not blame the Jews for Jesus's death. Instead, he claims, he agrees with members of the media, Jewish leaders, Christian scholars, and others who all wanted to make sure the film avoided pro-moting hate against Jewish people. Not everyone agrees he succeeded.

Gibson insists he merely followed scripture, which does not blame Jews for Christ's death. Instead, in all four Gospel stories, Jesus knew what was going to happen to him and predicted his own death—so he had a choice: he could have hidden or run away instead of allowing him-self to be captured. According to this line of thinking, Jesus himself was responsible for his death, not the Jewish authorities. Gibson also points out that Jesus himself was Jewish—so how, Gibson asks, can the movie be anti-Semitic, when it glorifies a Jew? Gibson goes on to say that he

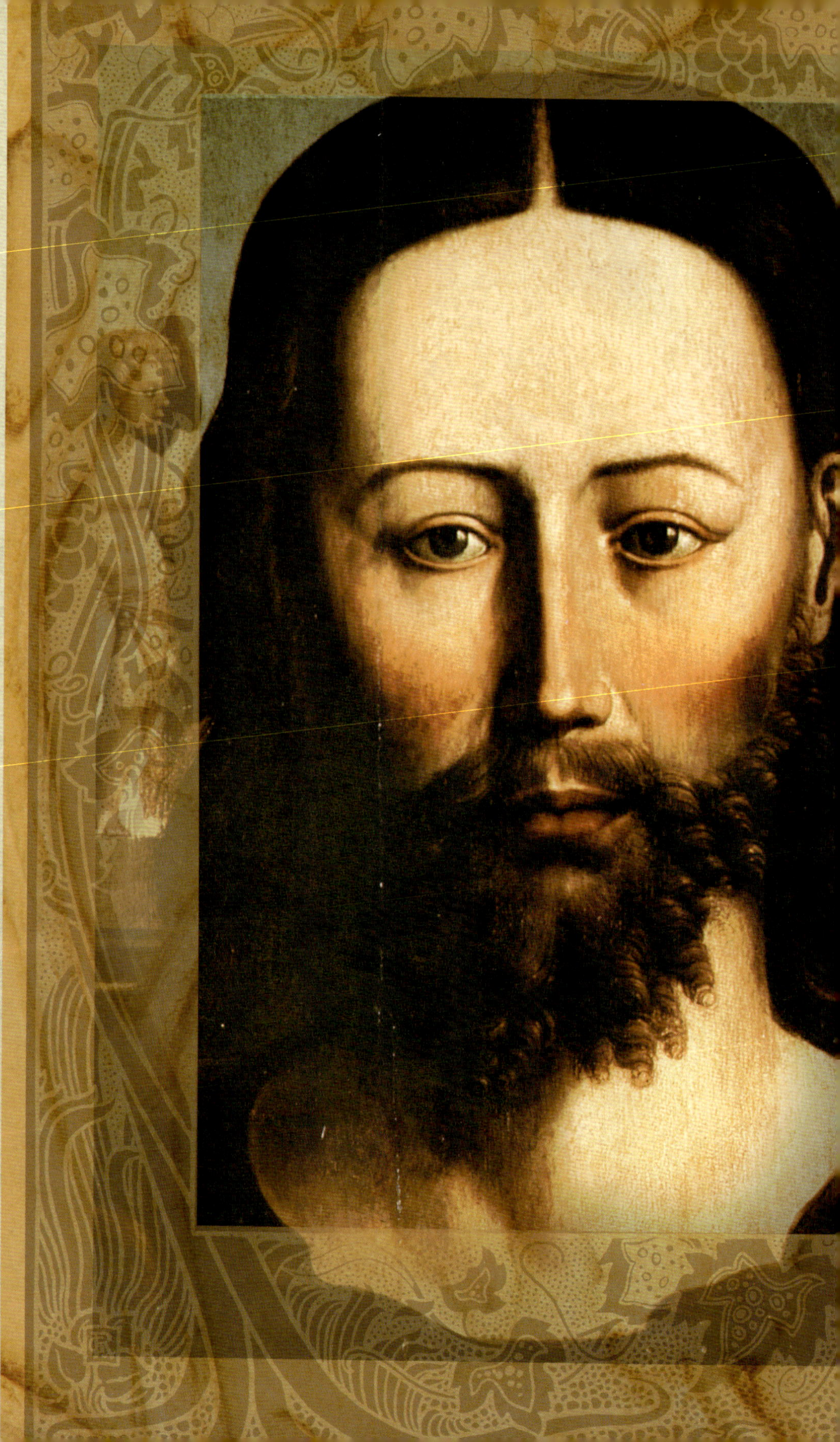

A TOOL FOR EVANGELISM

On the Web site Answers in Action, Gretchen Passantino claims that Gibson's movie is a powerful tool for convincing unbelievers to turn to Christianity. Jennfier Trafton of ChristianityToday.com agrees, saying:

> A play is more effective than a painting or even a sermon because it involves both the eye and the ear, both the illustration and the proclamation. It can convert those who could not be converted in any other way and move cold hearts to a new warmth of compassion and love for the suffering Messiah. Drama is a "living book," a picture that speaks, a sermon made concrete and immediate, a marriage of word and image.

Not all Christians agree with Passantino on this point. Many other people of faith see it from other perspectives: as a moving portrayal, as a work of art, or as a spiritual experience rather than a tool to bring about conversions.

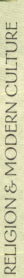

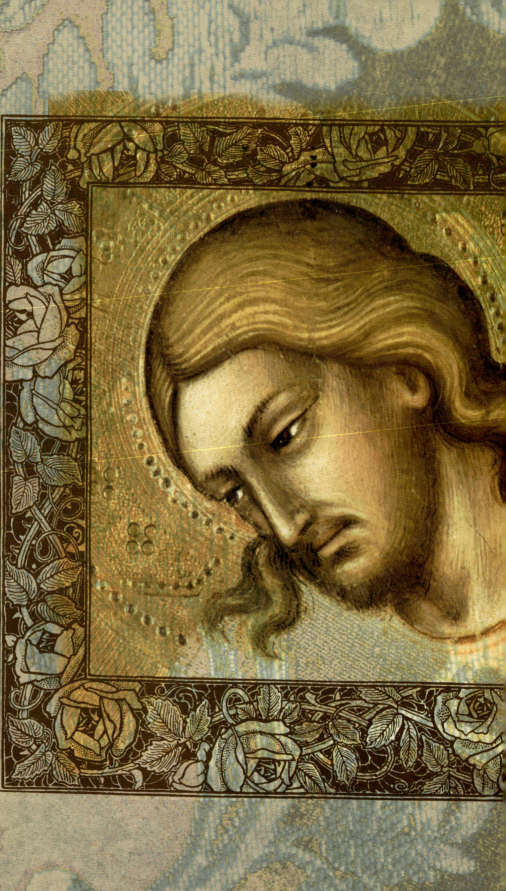

ANTI-SEMITISM AND THE PASSION

Many people—both Jews and Christians—are not convinced that Mel Gibson has adequately addressed the very real risk that his movie will inspire fresh waves of anti-Semitism. According to Abraham Foxman, national director of the Anti-Defamation League, "For almost 2,000 years in Western civilization, four words legitimized, rationalized, and fueled anti-Semitism: 'The Jews killed Christ.' . . . For hundreds of years those four words—acted out, spoken out, sermonized out—inspired and legitimized pogroms, inquisitions and expulsions."

believes everyone—no matter his or her religion—is responsible for putting the nails into Jesus's hands and feet. To make his point in the film, Gibson filmed his own hands nailing Jesus to the cross.

For many viewers, Mel Gibson's film was a big visual question: What if the historical Jesus truly suffered in this terrible way? What if he was not only a human but *paradoxically* also God's son? What spiritual effect would the visual experience of Jesus's story have on viewers? *The Passion of the Christ* seeks to create deep emotions in response to Christ's agony. Whether viewers agree that such an experience is valid or valuable, most would agree that Gibson succeeded: his graphic portrayal of Jesus's Passion is nearly overwhelming. Despite the film's controversy—perhaps even because of it—Gibson has brought the Passion back to the awareness of modern culture.

Chapter 2

MEDIA THAT ASKS, "WHAT IF?"

RELIGION & MODERN CULTURE

Teenager Joan Girardi approaches a bench at a bus stop in her hometown of Arcadia. A stranger makes room for her on the bench. Joan is minding her own business, but the stranger tries to strike up a conversation.

"They should put benches at all the bus stops. Make the world a better place, one tush at a time. What do you think, Joan?"

Why does this woman know her name? Strangely enough, Joan knows the answer right away: this stranger is God. She pauses to consider, then shakes her head and grins. "God says tush?"

As you can imagine, this is a strange experience for Joan, but she is getting used to various people who pop up and introduce themselves as God. At times, she questions her own sanity. Joan just wants to be a normal teenager, but fitting in as a teen is not easy when God keeps showing up in the forms of different people from all around the city of Arcadia.

"You always want something," Joan says to God at the bus stop. "What is it this time?"

"Since you're offering," replies God, "would you be a doll and get me a latte?"

"And God sayeth: 'Getteth me a coffee'?" quips Joan.

"Two sugars, please."

When Joan gets to the coffee stand on the street corner, three popular girls from school are there. She doesn't want to talk to them because they consider themselves on a higher social class than Joan. One of them, Dillan, begins to tease her. "Hey, nice bag. Bargain bin? K-Mart?"

Joan, as usual, is sarcastic: "And your heads, I assume, are from Mattel?"

Dillan retaliates by knocking Joan's bag onto the ground as she walks away from the coffee cart. Then as she crosses the street, Dillan trips, drops her coffee, and tries to pick it up. Joan notices a car rushing at Dillan and dives to save her life. Lying on the ground next to Dillan, Joan looks back to see the God-stranger getting on a bus without her latte.

Joan is a hero, and everyone in school and in the city is interested in her immediately. God visits Joan again: first as a trendy makeup artist while Joan is preparing to be interviewed at a news station, then in the girls' room in the form of a short freshman student. "You saved a life," says God. "Don't you want to get to know the life you saved?"

Joan does not get all the answers to her questions, but her questions lead her to the real reason God sent her to Dillan. The mean girl was

GLOSSARY

authoritarian: Having to do with blind submission to someone in authority.
conservative: Unwilling to consider new ideas; resistant to change.
orthodoxy: Conformity to accepted church doctrine and teachings.

so busy being popular that she never learned who she was or what she liked. She softens up and stops spending time with her shallow—but popular—friends, and Joan reluctantly becomes Dillan's friend. She changes Dillan's life by helping her find her own identity.

This popular television show *Joan of Arcadia* was inspired by the historic Joan of Arc, who struggled deeply with whether she was receiving messages from God. The religious leaders of her time doubted her. Today, just as in those times, questions can be intimidating to ask in churches, temples, or other religious groups. Popular culture can allow people to explore spiritual possibilities without ***authoritarian*** limitations.

Questions about important religious ideas have always been difficult to ask. Canadian folk singer Leonard Cohen explores many themes of spirituality and religion, and in one of his songs he sings about such difficult questions: "When they said: 'Repent!/Repent, repent!'/I wonder what they meant." The theme song for *Joan of Arcadia* goes: "What if

"What if God was one of us, just a slob like one of us?"

—*lyrics by singer Joan Osborne*

God was one of us?/Just a slob like one of us?/Just a stranger on the bus, trying to make his way home." This song by popular singer Joan Osborne asks a subtle but important question: "What if?"

The media provides open opportunities to consider the question of "What if?" In certain ways, *Joan of Arcadia* and *The Passion of the Christ* are asking the same questions: *What if God, the creator of the universe, was one of us? What if the Creator of the universe actually understands what we go through from personal experience?*

Joan of Arcadia's character asks us to consider what it would mean for God to be involved with teenagers on a daily basis. As a normal teenager, Joan is allowed to make her own choices about the answer to this question. She has a lot of unexplainable evidence to help her decide. Random people appear, seem to be speaking in God's voice, and tell her what God wants to tell her. "I'm just trying to show I care," says God in the form of the bus-stop stranger. She gets a bit choked up and motherly: "Because I do." And though Joan treats her a bit like a sarcastic teen treats a parent, she generally does what God asks her to do. God and Joan have an ongoing and developing relationship.

Although the show does not refer directly to Jesus by name, it is interesting to make a comparison. In the Bible, Jesus was a human, just *one of us*, yet Jesus does and says things that show that he may be more than just human. Therefore, Christians consider Jesus to be God at the same time. What if Jesus is not only a character in an ancient religious story but a way to understand God as caring about young people and old people alike?

HollywoodJesus.com gives the show's official list of guidelines, "The Ten Commandments of *Joan of Arcadia*":

1. God cannot directly intervene.
2. Good and evil exist.
3. God can never identify one religion as being right.
4. The job of every human is to fulfill his or her own nature.
5. Everyone is allowed to say "no" to God, including Joan.
6. God is not bound by time.
7. God . . . does not possess human personality.
8. God talks to everyone all the time in different ways.
9. God's plan is what is good for us, not what is good for Him.
10. God's purpose for talking to Joan, and everyone, is to get her (us) to recognize the interconnectedness of all things. God expects us to learn from our experiences. However, the exact nature of God is a mystery, and the mystery can never be solved.

"Homer [Simpson] wants a hair-restoring formula to work: 'Dear God, give the bald guy a break!' It does work, but only for a short time, and it turns Homer's life upside down."

—*Mark I. Pinsky*, The Gospel According to The Simpsons

WHAT IF JESUS IS MORE OPEN-MINDED THAN HIS FOLLOWERS?

Saved (2004) is a film that asks, *What if believing in cardboard cutout or abstract Jesus isn't enough?* What if everyday reality, sex, crisis of faith, teen pregnancy, and gossip are all issues God can understand? *Saved* begins with a monologue by the popular teenage main character, Mary: "It seems like I've been saved all my life."

Saved gives the viewers a humorous look inside a Christian high school with a forty-foot (12-meter) wooden cut-out of Jesus in front. Students deal with real-life issues adults tried to hide or downplay. Mary's boyfriend turns out to be gay, and she gives up her virginity to him to help him become straight. Obviously, this doesn't work.

The adults in this film care deeply about these young adults, but they don't know what to do. The boyfriend's parents send him away to a school they hope will cure him of his homosexuality. When Mary finds out she's pregnant, she can't even talk to her loving mother about it. All of a sudden, Mary doesn't feel as "saved" as she had before. She loses her snobby religious friends when they learn of her sinful ways. Depressed, Mary ends up alone before finding new friends: a Jewish atheist girl and a boy in a wheelchair. Mary is thrust into a spiritual crisis: where is God at a time like this? She puts on black glasses and sneaks into a woman's center for help. She has very few choices and is desperate. At one point,

A MEDIA THAT ASKS, "WHAT IF?"

41

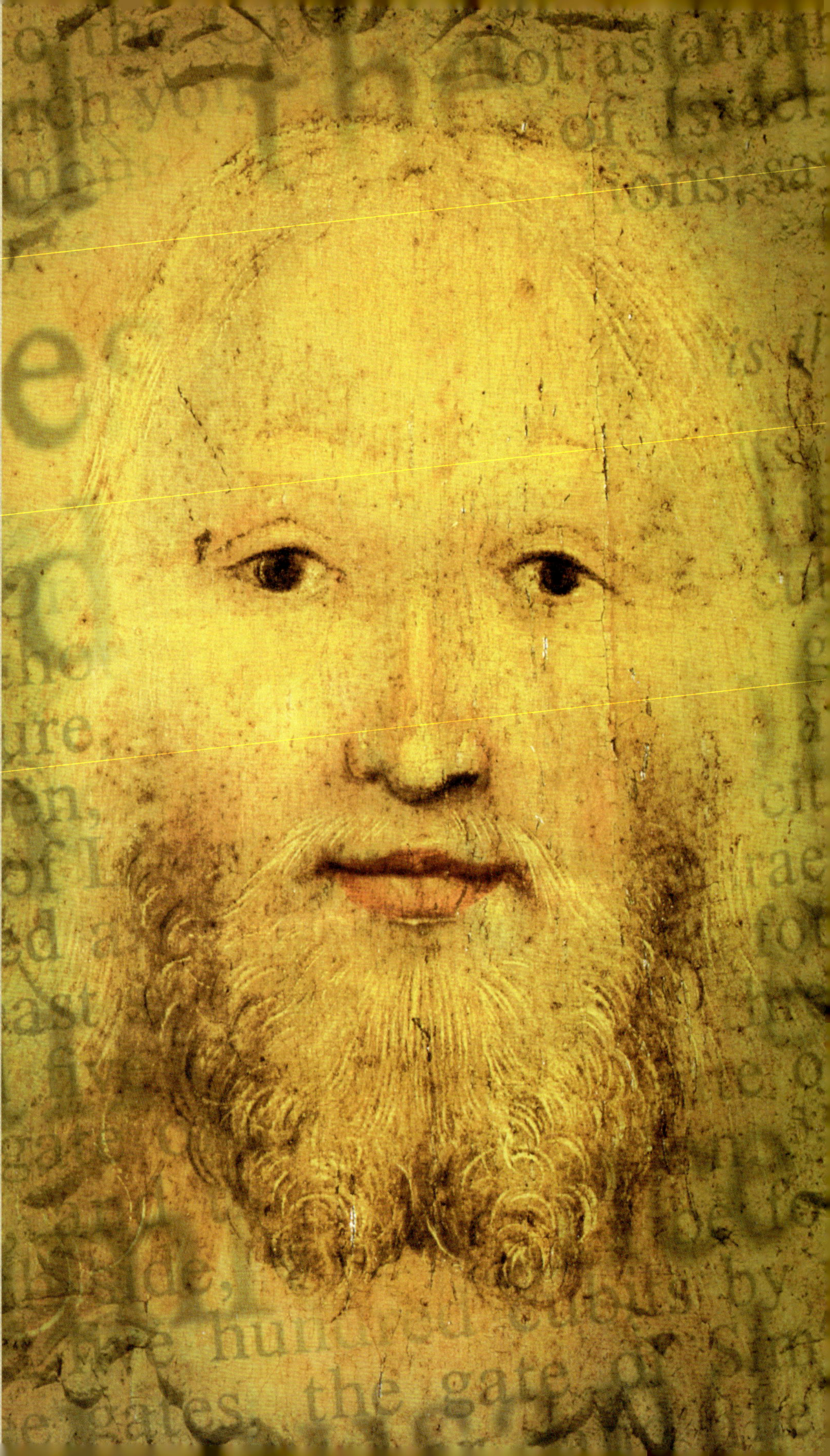

Mary stops in front of a church, walks up to the cross, and prays with passion using only profanities. Could God deal with that? Could he understand her even though she was swearing?

At the end of the film, various relationships are set right. Mary's snobby ex-best friend gets angry and runs her SUV into the cardboard Jesus, then is embraced by her peers. Her mom and other adults finally listen to the teens. Mary's homosexual friend is awkwardly accepted for who he is.

WHAT IF JESUS HAS A GREAT SENSE OF HUMOR?

The raunchy television comedy series *South Park* is nothing like the shows mentioned previously in this chapter. It asks: What if Jesus was a normal guy in the neighborhood? South Park Jesus just wants to get along in his life. The other characters keep bothering him, asking him important questions at football games that he can't seem to answer. In one episode, Jesus gets into a fight with Santa Claus over Christmas. *South Park* creators go the furthest in making Jesus more human and never showing him as the Son of God. There are episodes that ask the questions: What if Jesus were fat? What if Jesus were happy all the time? These questions might be difficult to ask at a neighborhood church. On *South Park*, you won't get a serious answer.

Churches tend to be more ***conservative*** than the popular media. By definition, most churches are rooted in the past, concerned with issues of ***orthodoxy*** and biblical accuracy. Television and movies have no such restraints. These forms of the media can form an interface between popular culture and religion, a place where questions can be asked about Christianity. Television and movies may not provide answers—but the questions themselves stimulate thought and reflection.

Chapter 3

JESUS IN POPULAR MUSIC

RELIGION & MODERN CULTURE

Kanye West is an unusual rapper. For one thing, he wears preppy sweaters instead of oversized jerseys. In an interview for *Spin* magazine, Kanye said he likes to think that almost anyone can identify with him. His first CD, *The College Dropout*, broke the hip-hop music mold with lyrics about self-doubt and insecurity. Jon Caramanica wrote in a 2004 *Spin* article that, "Twelve months ago, Kanye West was a highly re-garded hip-hop producer recovering from a near-fatal car accident: not someone you'd expect to make the most important record of 2004."

According to West himself, the most important thing he did that year was record a song called "Jesus Walks," which he showcased in three different videos. In these videos, Jesus walks along with a Ku Klux Klan (KKK) member, drug dealers, and various other "sinners," including West himself.

One "Jesus Walks" video shows West as a rapping preacher in a church, with a choir singing in the background. During the sermon, an alcoholic, a thug, and a prostitute all "come forward" to meet Christ at the front altar of the church. "That was the first one he did," said his mother, Donda West, in an interview with *Relevant* magazine. "Kanye is so very passionate about this song, and he's also a perfectionist. He wanted to say something in these videos to reach people, and you can really relate to this video if you are from that tradition."

A second, more edgy, video shows the story of KKK members burning a cross, doves flying into air, and drug dealers running from the law. Mrs. West said, "It's healing . . . for all people who have been persecuted in a direct way, like racism. When you see Jesus even walking with a Klan member, who is so entrenched in hate, you can see that redemption is for everyone."

According to *Relevant* magazine, West was the director of the third video. The bushy-bearded Jesus is hanging around the rapper for a regular day in his hometown of Chicago. This video is less flashy and shows that Kanye takes his song personally. Mrs. West continues in the interview, "Jesus taps on the empty refrigerator and it becomes filled with food."

Mrs. West goes on to explain that her son is not a religious rapper:

To me, Kanye is saying with a devout faith, you can have faith as far as the eye can see. I think he'd like to see more people have this faith. That's why he says if you see me in the club, scream, "Jesus Walks."

pagan: Having to do with pre-Christian religions that worshipped the Earth and/or some form of the Goddess.

At the 2005 Grammy Award show, Kanye West won three awards, including "Best Rap Song" for "Jesus Walks."

JESUS IN POPULAR SONGS

Kanye West is not the only artist who connects Christian faith with his music. Moreover, not all popular music that refers to Jesus is connected to churches or other religious organizations. With his first album, Kanye West joins musicians such as U2, Creed, P.O.D., Moby, and Lauryn Hill. On her 2001 post-9/11 remembrance album *America: A Tribute to Heroes*, Faith Hill inspired hope in God's future for the earth through the song "There Will Come a Day." Rapper Twista and R & B singer Faith Evans do the same thing in their song "Hope" from the *Coach Carter* film soundtrack. U2's spiritual rock music is among the most popular and influential in the world. These musicians are all influenced directly or indirectly by Gospel music; they do not give up their popularity in order to tell people what they believe.

47

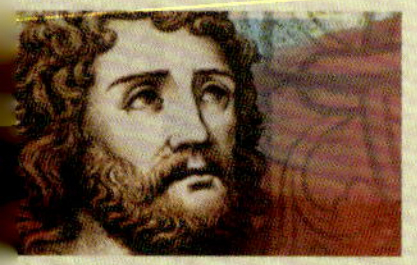

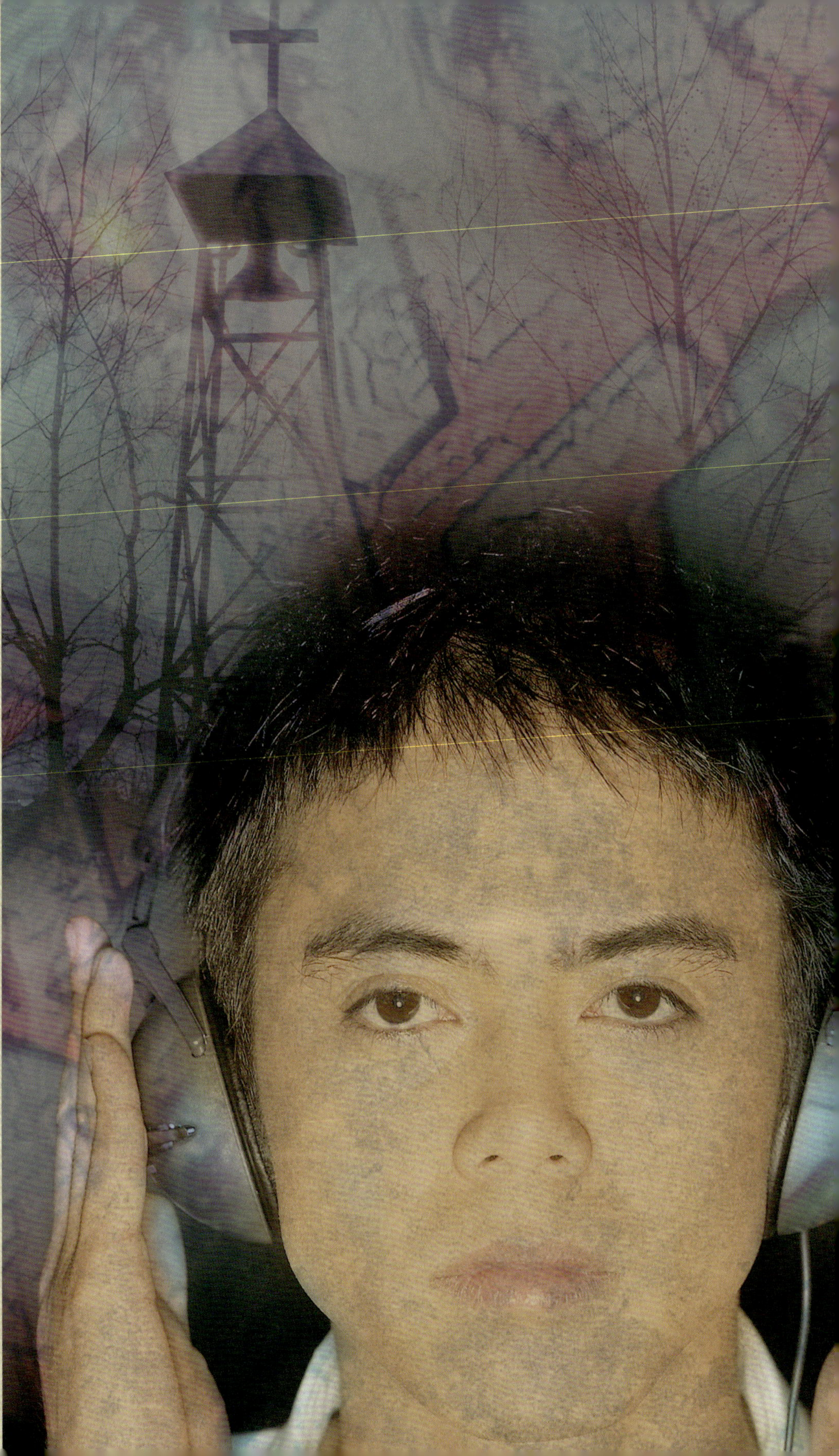

"My music tries to say how I really feel, and I hope it [reflects] how black people feel in the United States."

—*Jazz musician Max Roach, 1963*

Faith and music go together; music moves us, makes us dance. A song can cause us to remember a girlfriend or boyfriend or a good time with friends. Music inspires us and helps us to believe. Music is important to us because it connects with our feelings. As we go about our lives, we may hum songs that match our moods as if we are living through our own musicals. Some of us don't pay attention to the words in our favorite songs; we just love the tunes. Sometimes we play painful or angry songs because that is how we feel, and at other times we focus on song lyrics that are poetic in nature.

No matter what kind of music we listen to, there is a good chance that the music we like connects to our personal spirituality. The variety of spiritual expressions in popular music is as diverse as the multitude of music genres. Both popular Christian artists and nonreligious artists use Jesus as subject matter. Songs about Jesus—by both kinds of artists—can interact with emotions and help create meaning.

CHRISTIAN MUSIC IN POPULAR CULTURE

Some popular music focuses completely on Jesus. Christian musicians produce music through strictly Christian record companies and write music about Jesus for church services. Since many North Americans are Christians, this kind of music sells well.

While most people enjoy whatever music moves them, some religious people see a strong division between church music and secular

music containing religious themes. Even though popular culture has some roots in the Christian church, "The relationship between pop music and religion has not been pretty," writes Barry Taylor. "Christians have burned records labeled demonic and picketed concerts deemed satanic." Robert Palmer notes that, "A 1958 Catholic youth center newsletter urged kids to 'smash records you possess which present a *pagan* culture and a pagan way of life.'" Even today, some church youth groups have what they call "CD Crosses." The youth are encouraged to nail their secular compact discs to large wooden crosses. However, these days, far fewer Christians are completely biased against the popular music culture. Many Christians are, on the contrary, interested in the spirituality of all kinds of music.

In the 1970s, North American culture was changing, led by the spiritual philosophies of many popular musicians. In 1973, the popular musical *Jesus Christ Superstar* retold the Passion story. The Doobie Brothers sang a popular song called "Jesus Is Just Alright with Me," inspired by a hippie community called the Jesus People.

Before—and even during—those days, many Christians felt they should not be popular singers because such jobs might not please God. Being a religious leader was more important than being a popular singer. Christian music stayed in the church to avoid contamination by "the world." However, at the same time, many popular musicians were becoming "Jesus People," who struggled with how to become part of church culture while remaining professional musicians.

Bob Dylan converted to Christianity in 1979; around the same time, so did a handful of other famous rockers who all decided to bring their new spirituality into their music. Because Dylan's songs were poetic and truthful, fans considered him a prophet, someone who could see the truth in the world better than most people. Dylan said that year, "I told you,'The Times They Are A-Changin,' and they did. I said the answer is 'Blowin' in the Wind' and it was. I'm telling you that Jesus is coming back, and He is."

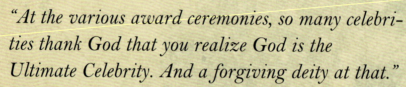

> *"At the various award ceremonies, so many celebrities thank God that you realize God is the Ultimate Celebrity. And a forgiving deity at that."*
> —Paul Krassner

Things changed again when the '80s began. Madonna, whose name comes from a Catholic name for Jesus's mother, was one of the biggest musicians in popular culture. She was famous for wearing crosses as fashion accessories. Perhaps one of her most controversial videos was "Like a Prayer," which featured Madonna having a love relationship with a statue of a black Jesus that came to life with a kiss.

In the '90s, popular music began to reflect much spiritual doubt. The band R.E.M. had a hit song "Losing My Religion," and Nirvana sang "Smells Like Teen Spirit," a teen anthem, although the title reportedly refers to a brand of deodorant. Meanwhile, '90s Christian bands were trying to take their religious messages to the secular radio stations to bring hope and belief back to the forefront. These bands were part of a new genre called Christian Contemporary Music (CCM).

A few CCM artists achieved success with secular and religious fans. These were known as "crossover" performers, because their popularity crossed over two different markets. CCM crossover performers like Michael W. Smith and Amy Grant were successful because of the emotions and struggles they shared with their fans. These two even had videos on MTV, which was new for Christian artists at that time. Other crossover bands of the '90s were DC Talk, The Newsboys, P.O.D., and Sixpence None the Richer.

According to CanadianChristianity.com in 2001, "Contemporary Christian Music has experienced substantial growth. From humble beginnings, it currently generates annual sales in excess of $750 million, outselling jazz and classical recordings."

SPIRITUAL MUSICAL ROOTS

Classical music began as both spiritual music and popular music in Europe. In its beginnings, Christianity was so prevalent that popular music was presented as a way to worship God. Hymns became popular when Protestant Christians wanted to teach about God through music that moves the soul.

Both jazz and gospel music were born when music and faith combined within repressed communities. Jazz and gospel singers gave listeners hope for freedom. They worshipped God with faithful voices and instruments. Reggae, hip-hop, and country music all have similar religious roots. Today, music is cut and pasted out of these varied styles, connecting with listeners in new spiritual ways.

MEANING IN POPULAR GOSPEL MUSIC

Many black musical artists were trained in churches where they sang gospel. This form of religious music is rooted in African American history and culture. Robert Darden, author of *People Get Ready: A New History of Black Gospel Music*, describes early gospel musicians' connection to both faith and musical talent:

Sallie Martin, Mahalia Jackson and Willie Mae Ford Smith all believed in letting the Holy Ghost have Its way; each of them made this belief performatively obvious in her singing. The new choruses, under these vocalists' careful tutelage, thus learned more than just new tunes. They also received training in the freedom and faith of singing in the Spirit.

Especially in the African American Holiness churches, "experience pervades all description of worship and performance." Each service, each song, is designed to invite the presence of the Holy Spirit, the third member of the Christian church's "Holy Trinity." What Jackson was apparently able to do better than virtually all singers before or after her, according to numerous eyewitness accounts, was take listeners to a place where they could feel the "touch" of the Holy Spirit.

Today, the African American community's deep spiritual roots take on new musical expressions. Tupac Shakur, for instance, has left a legacy of meaningful rap that has inspired a generation of artists. Though his lyrics are too crude for the "polite public," they connect with many oppressed people through emotion and meaning. In "Letter 2 My Unborn," he raps,

In case I don't make it/. . . Since I got one life to live/God forgive my sins/. . . My only friend is my misery/want my revenge for the agony that they did to me/See my life ain't promised, but it's gonna get better/Hope you understand my love letter/To my unborn child/. . . I want to go in peace when I gotta die/ Lord can you hear me?

This song is from the album *Until the End of Time,* which carries parental advisories for language. The rapper's meaning shows suffering

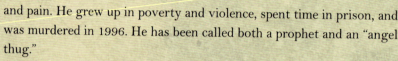

and pain. He grew up in poverty and violence, spent time in prison, and was murdered in 1996. He has been called both a prophet and an "angel thug."

Gospel origins also influence country music. In both Canada and the United States, country music becomes more popular with time. George Canyon was the number-one country singer in Canada in 2005 who took home three prizes in Canada's 2005 East Coast Music Awards for his debut album *One Good Friend*. Canyon's belief in Christ is apparent in his music.

Another band known for Gospel influences and meaningful lyrics is U2. U2 began in Ireland in the 1980s. Three of the four band members found faith in Jesus when they were young. They eventually had to leave their church because they had a disagreement over how to handle the band's fame with secular audiences. The lead singer, Bono (Paul Hewson), criticizes foolishness within Christian music and churches, but he uses Bible stories and Jesus's teachings in many songs to convey deep spiritual searching.

Their 2000 album *All That You Can't Leave Behind* has a song called "Grace," which goes: "Grace, she takes the blame/She covers the shame/Removes the stain/. . . Grace, it's the name for a girl/It's also a thought that changed the world." When Bono accepted several awards for that album, he credited God with U2's success. In his usual poetic way, he described the spiritual way that U2 waits for God to inspire them: "We depend on God walking through the room, more than most. And God has walked through the room on our record and I want to give thanks. Amen."

Gospel is deeply rooted in the popular music of this new millennium; many believe that through this medium, Jesus walks wherever Jesus wants to walk. Award-winning T-Bone Burnett's faith shows strongly in the bluegrass music featured in the film *O Brother, Where Art Thou?* Lenny Kravitz's song "Dig In" includes lines like, "When the mountain is high,/Just look up to the sky/Ask God to teach you/Then persevere

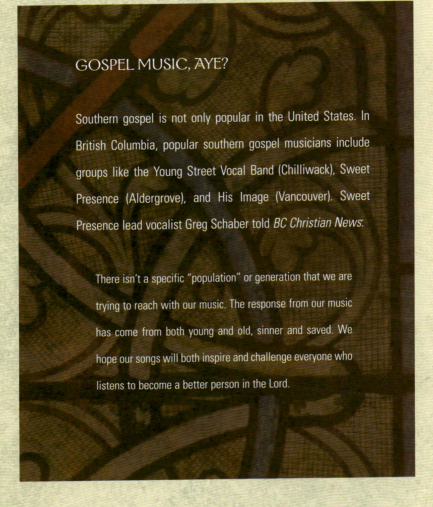

GOSPEL MUSIC, AYE?

Southern gospel is not only popular in the United States. In British Columbia, popular southern gospel musicians include groups like the Young Street Vocal Band (Chilliwack), Sweet Presence (Aldergrove), and His Image (Vancouver). Sweet Presence lead vocalist Greg Schaber told *BC Christian News*:

There isn't a specific "population" or generation that we are trying to reach with our music. The response from our music has come from both young and old, sinner and saved. We hope our songs will both inspire and challenge everyone who listens to become a better person in the Lord.

RELIGION & MODERN CULTURE

with a smile." Destiny's Child's Grammy-winning song "Survivor" includes the lyric "I'm not going to compromise my Christianity."

Mel Gibson used film to express his spiritual beliefs, but clearly, popular music is a cultural vehicle for religious ideas as well. Music and television programs are not the only forms of popular media that have been influenced by religion and spirituality, however, nor is Gibson's movie the only one touched by the Passion of Christ. Other films also deal with Jesus, and their strong visual representations provide culturally relevant interpretations of the Gospel story.

Chapter 4

THE GOD/MAN
OF THE MOVIES

RELIGION & MODERN CULTURE

Jesus's friend Lazarus, who lived in the town of Bethany, became deathly ill, and so his sisters sent a messenger requesting Jesus to come and cure him. Although Jesus cared deeply for Lazarus, Mary, and Martha, he chose not to come to Bethany at that time. When Jesus did go to Lazarus's town days later, Lazarus had died. Jesus and Martha had the following conversation, as recorded in *The Message*, a modern version of the Bible written by Eugene Peterson:

"Master, if you'd been here, my brother wouldn't have died. Even now, I know that whatever you ask God he will give you."

Jesus said, "Your brother will be raised up."

Martha replied, "I know that he will be raised up in the resurrection at the end of time."

"You don't have to wait for the End. I am, right now, Resurrection and Life. The one who believes in me, even though he or she dies, will live. And everyone who lives believing in me does not ultimately die at all.

Jesus then went with the sisters to Lazarus's tomb, where he commanded onlookers to roll away the tombstone. They objected that the corpse would stink, but Jesus insisted that they do so. Then Jesus called to the dead man, "Come forth!" And Lazarus walked out of his tomb—miraculously restored to life

Jesus shows passion for his friend in this scene. He cries at the death of his friend and endures criticism from Lazarus's sisters for not showing up on time. When Jesus films bring scenes like this to life, Christ's human emotions help viewers to see him as a good man willing to experience pain out of love for people. However, for many Christians, Jesus was not only a good man and a prophet, but he was also God in the flesh. He is called both "the Son of Man" and "the Son of God" in the Gospels. Some films about Jesus focus on his human nature, and other films emphasize his *divinity*. Mel Gibson focused on Christ's divinity.

You might say that Gibson created a new Passion story for our times—but other filmmakers have done this before. The world-famous *Jesus* film project, for example, was written almost entirely from the Gospel of Luke, setting a new standard for showing the entire text of one book of scripture in a motion picture. The creators changed little about the story, so a viewer could actually read along in Luke's Gospel while listening to the narrator. Since this Protestant *evangelical* film

GLOSSARY

divinity: The state of being divine—in other words, being God.

evangelical: Having to do with a form of Christianity that holds the Bible in high regard, while emphasizing the necessity for a personal relationship with Christ in order to achieve eternal salvation.

Gethsemane: The garden outside Jerusalem described in the Gospel of Mark as the scene of Christ's prayer and spiritual struggle before the crucifixion, followed by his arrest.

Incarnation: God's embodiment in a human being in the person of Jesus of Nazareth; the word's literal meaning in Latin is "the taking on of flesh."

prodigal son: A parable told by Jesus, in which a runaway son is welcomed home by a forgiving father, the father symbolizing God, while the son is a metaphor for human beings who have turned away from God's presence.

was released in 1979, it has been translated into hundreds of languages and shown to groups around the world. A more recent movie, *The Gospel of John* (2003), takes a similar approach, using another Gospel for its script.

In Jesus films, Christ not only suffers as a human; he also feels emotions and interacts as a human. We see, for example, that Jesus had

"I want to show the humanity of Christ as well as the divine aspect. It's a rendering that for me is very realistic and as close as possible to what I perceive the truth to be."

—*Mel Gibson*

normal interactions and relationships. He was fond of children, spent time with unlikely friends, and taught the twelve men known as his disciples; he also ate dinner with people outside his social class, turned water into wine at parties, and treated women with more respect than others of his time. Some filmmakers want to show how human Jesus really was by adding even more human features to the biblical stories of Jesus's life. They use their own imaginations and creativity to interact with the Gospel stories.

THE LAST TEMPTATION OF CHRIST

Many religious leaders sharply criticized some films for making Jesus too human. One of these films is *The Last Temptation of Christ* (1988), which explored Jesus's nature as a divine being living as a suffering human. Both the Catholic director, Martin Scorsese, and the Protestant screenwriter, Paul Schrader, said they based the film on a novel by Nikos Kazantzakis rather than the Gospels.

The last temptation referred to in the movie's title occurs when Jesus wants to avoid going through the Passion in order to live a normal life. In the film, Jesus is portrayed as having sexual desires and wanting to marry his friend, Mary Magdalene. The film shows his internal temptation as a long fantasy that takes up about half an hour. In the end, the

Jesus of Montreal is a film about a priest who hires young Montreal actors to create a new Passion play in the form of a stage drama. The production asks the question: "What would Jesus look like today?" It is a satire that shows ways the Passion story may have been distorted through history. The actors use Mount Royal as an outdoor stage. They impress the crowd but have changed the story too much from tradition, so a priest is uncomfortable. The film is partly about challenging the normal view of Jesus in art and film. Peter T. Chattaway writes that in most Jesus films, "Audiences think they have seen it all before." *Jesus of Montreal* reminds us that each Jesus film has something unique to say, and each provides a different cultural slant on the Gospel.

temptation is only a fantasy—but many Christians were uncomfortable with the idea that Christ might have experienced such a human temptation.

Some churchgoers thought the movie's fantasy portrayed Jesus as a sinner. They assumed that it was an attack on the divinity of Jesus and on Christian faith, claiming that disobedience to God—even in a fantasy—was contrary to Christ's nature as it is described in the Bible; consequently, they boycotted the film. Other religious people did not feel the film threatened their image of Christ; instead, they thought the film

65

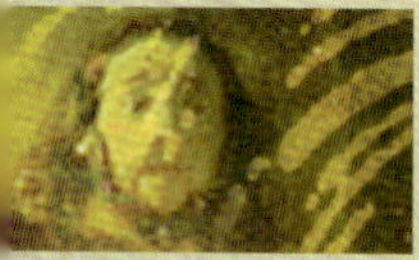

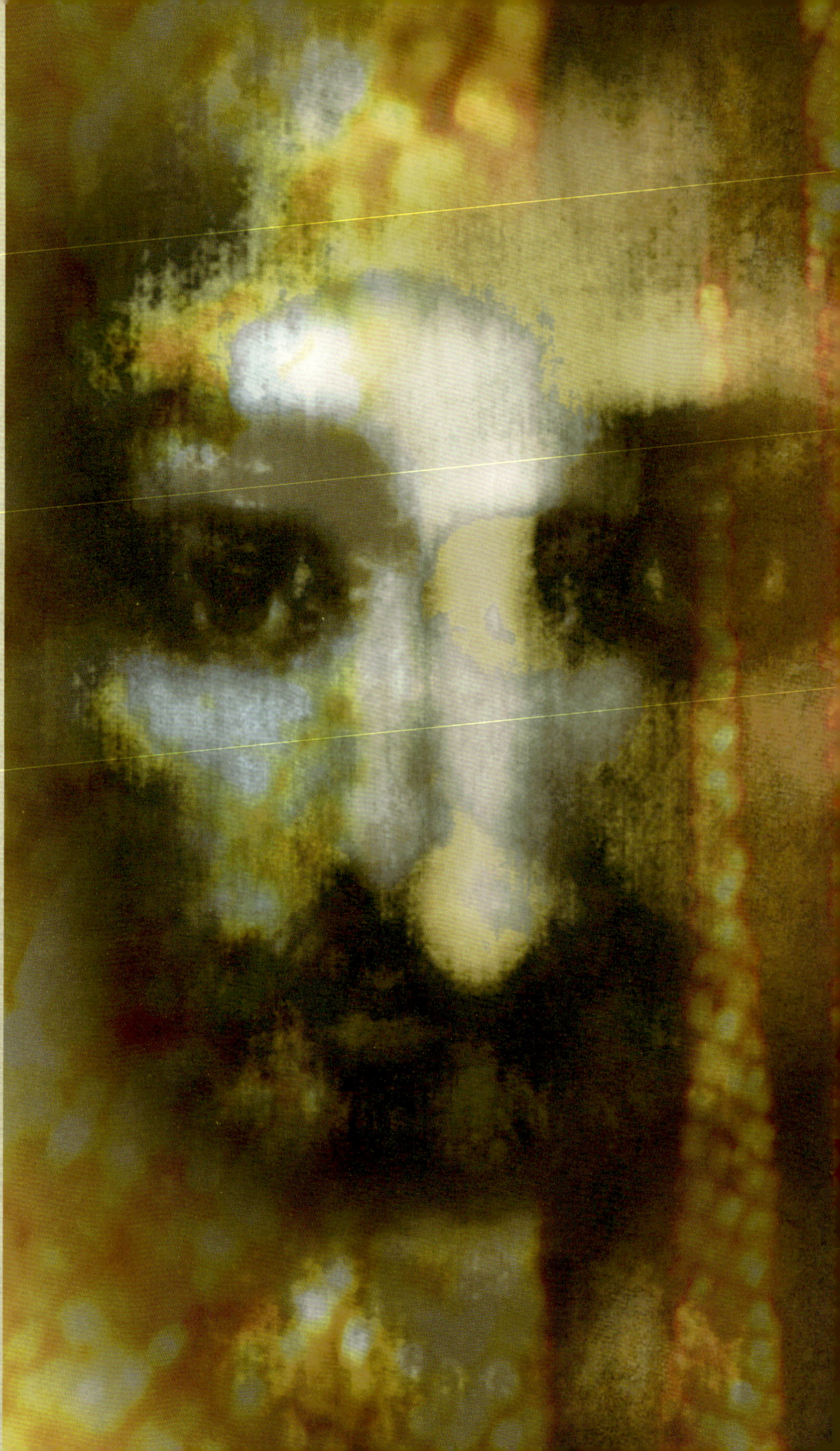

> *"It comes down to the fact that conservative Christians take the portrayal of Jesus personally. It matters religiously to them that Jesus be portrayed 'faithfully' from the scriptures, that he be 'God' on screen."*
>
> —*April DeConick*

was good because it showed Jesus had all the temptations any person might have—so he can understand what it really means to be human. Still others were simply interested in the questions the movie brought to life about the nature of Christ. For these people, questions in and of themselves are valuable ways of investigating the spiritual life—while others believe that certain questions can be sacrilegious or irreverent.

Meanwhile, the film's director, Martin Scorsese, insisted he was a genuine believer with deep theological interests. He said that both the film and the Nikos Kazantzakis novel on which it was based were explorations of the meaning of the **Incarnation**. He intended his movie to explore the question: what did it mean for Christ to be both fully human and fully God?

Jesus in *The Last Temptation* wrestles with self-doubt and temptation. He struggles with his own identity and his mission from God, and only on the cross, as he is dying, does he finally commit himself totally to his calling. This divine mission, from Scorsese's perspective, has little to do with teaching, healing, or living a life based on love; instead, Scorsese indicates that Jesus's most important purpose on earth was to unite the human and divine. The movie suggests that it is only in Christ's final acceptance of death and resurrection that his mission is fulfilled. As a result, the film says very little about the practical day-to-day implications of living out one's faith while interacting with the other people in one's life. Its questions have more to do with personal identity, the meaning of spirituality at a very private rather than a social level.

Another film that emphasizes Jesus's humanity is the earlier film *Jesus Christ Superstar*, which was originally produced in the 1970s as a rock opera, first in London and then on Broadway. A remake of this film is expected in 2006. The original film is packed with the arts of the time: it is a musical with 1970s pastel-colored costumes and simple art. In *Superstar*, Jesus walks through the scene as one of the people, rather than as a high and mighty God. The other characters give him both their love and scorn in passionate songs.

The most famous of these songs, "Jesus Christ Superstar," asks the movie's central question: "Do you think you're what they say you are?" Mary Magdalene, Herod, Pilate, and the mob are all constantly asking Jesus who he is. In this movie, Judas, who has traditionally been portrayed as the evil betrayer of Christ, acts as a spokesperson for those who are genuinely puzzled about Jesus's identity. *Jesus Christ Superstar* provides no answers about Jesus's identity; it only asks question after question.

The Jesus portrayed in *Superstar* is human enough to be frightened at **Gethsemane**. In that scene, Jesus asks God:

Why then am I scared to finish what I started,
What you started—I didn't start it.

The Jesus portrayed here even dares to criticize and question God.

Like *The Last Temptation of Christ, Jesus Christ Superstar* is willing to risk offense in a way that many other Jesus films avoid. The movie's creators do not care if they offend church leaders or devout Christians. Instead, they courageously and honestly interact with their own doubts and questions about the person of Jesus Christ. Some people were in fact

69

RELIGION & MODERN CULTURE

offended by *Superstar*. Others, however, gained a new emotional experience of Jesus's humanity that they felt had spiritual value in itself.

But if some conservative Christians were offended by *Jesus Christ Superstar* because of its depiction of a human Jesus, these Christians were even more upset by the movie's ending. *Superstar* ends with the crucifixion. Once Jesus is dead, the actors return home on a bus, deep in sorrowful thought—and then the credits role in silence. In the play version of *Jesus Christ Superstar*, the actor playing Jesus always returned for the curtain call, often dressed in a new, glittering costume. The film, however, lacks even a hint of the resurrection. Instead, the film's many questions are left ringing in the viewers' ears as they file out of the theater, their somber mood often paralleling that of the actors' in the final scene.

GODSPELL

Godspell tells a far different story. In this movie, also produced in the 1970s, the focus is on Jesus's joy and divinity, rather than on his sadness and humanity. Despite this different slant, however, in its own way, *Godspell*'s stance on the Gospels is as radical as *Superstar*'s.

"The Church takes itself much too seriously. It has to learn to laugh at itself sometimes. I think if Jesus were here today, he would be moving and acting like this," said Stephan Nathan, one of the actors who played Jesus in the original play, referring to *Godspell*'s laughter, dance, and music. This movie sought to shake Christians out of their staid and proper pews; its creators wanted to present viewers with a brand-new perspective of who Jesus is and what he means to the modern-day world.

The movie is a kaleidoscope of color, song, and movement, as the actors dance through the scenes costumed like Raggedy-Ann clowns. The Gospel stories come to life in a series of parodies, gags, music-hall routines, charades, puns, and pantomimes. Papier-mâché flowers magically

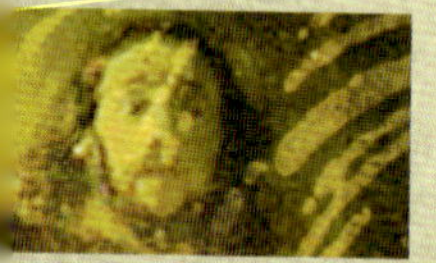

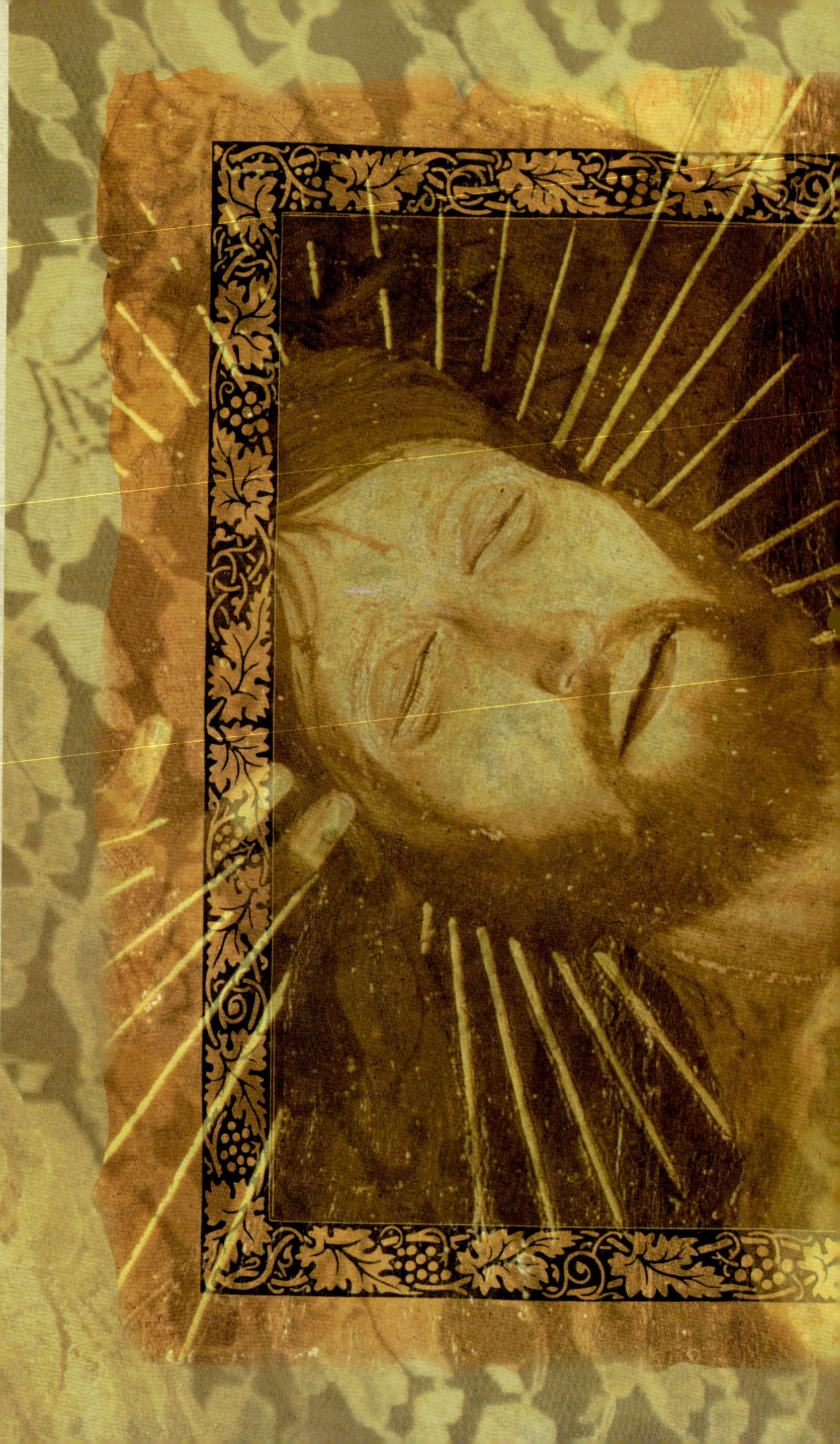

JESUS FILMS THROUGH HISTORY

The Passion Play of
Oberammergau (1898)

The Life and Passion of Christ
(1908)

From the Manger to the Cross
(1912)

The Last Supper (1914)

Intolerance (1916)

Christus (1917)

Leaves from Satan's Book
(Denmark, 1922)

I.N.R.I. (Germany, 1923)

The Passion Play (Germany,
1924)

The King of Kings (1927)

Jesus of Nazareth (1928)

Golgotha (1935)

Mary Magdeline (1946)

Quo Vadis (1951)

The Westminster Passion Play
(1951)

The Robe (1953)

The Power of Resurection (1958)

Ben-Hur (1959)

King of Kings (1961)

Barabbas (1962)

Pontius Pilate (1964)

The Greatest Story Ever Told
(1965)

The Redeemer (Spain, 1966)

The Gospel According to St.
Matthew (1966)

Black Jesus (Italy, 1968)

Jesus Christ Superstar (1973)

Godspell (1973)

The Gospel Road (1973)

Jesus of Nazareth (1977)

Jesus (1979)

Monty Python's Life of Brian
(1979)

The Last Temptation of Christ
(1988)

Jesus of Montreal (1989)

Jesus (2000)

The Miracle Maker (2000)

The Gospel of John (2003)

The Passion of the Christ (2004)

RELIGION & MODERN CULTURE

appear during Christ's sermon on the lilies of the field; money rains down as the **prodigal son** is reprimanded; and party favors explode at unlikely moments, catching the audience continually by surprise.

When *Godspell*'s author, John-Michael Tebelak, was asked why he wrote the original play on which the movie is based, he replied:

I had been working on my master's thesis for Carnegie Tech's School of Drama but put it aside . . . [and] went to the Easter Vigil service at the Anglican Cathedral in Pittsburgh. It was snowing, and I was aware of the proper setting for a religious experience. But the people in the church seemed bored, and the clergymen seemed to be hurrying to get it over with. I left with the feeling that, rather than rolling the rock away from the Tomb, they were piling more on. . . . The Church has become so dour and pessimistic; it has to reclaim its joy and hope. I see *Godspell* as a celebration of life.

The word "godspell" is Old English for *gospel*, and Tebelak wanted to create a drama that would remind viewers of the medieval plays that made the Gospel story into a popular entertainment form. (See page 25 for more about these plays.) Unlike the creators of *The Last Temptation* and *Superstar,* Tebelak was not so much asking questions as he was hoping to inspire some answers. In his own words, he was seeking to "weave God's spell over the audience."

What *Superstar* and *Godspell* did for the popular culture of the 1970s, *The Passion of the Christ* seeks to do for the first decade of the twenty-first century—bring the story of Jesus into mainstream thought and consciousness. And since we live in a world that focuses on buying and selling, it's inevitable that Jesus would also end up in stores and other markets.

Chapter 5

JESUS IN THE MARKETPLACE

In a local bookstore in 2004, a teenage boy picks up a copy of *The Da Vinci Code* by Dan Brown. The boy notes that in the preface, the author claims that certain descriptions in the book are factual. He's not sure if he trusts that since the book is technically fiction, but he thinks to himself, *What if*? As he stands in the aisle of the bookstore, he begins reading the prologue:

Louvre Museum, Paris. 10:46 P.M.—Renowned curator Jacques Sauniere staggered through the vaulted archway of the museum's Grand Gallery. He lunged for the nearest painting he could see, a Caravaggio. Grabbing the gilded frame, the seventy-six-year-old man heaved the masterpiece toward himself until it tore from the wall and Sauniere collapsed backward in a heap beneath the canvas.

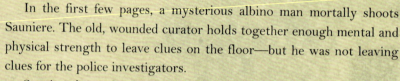

In the first few pages, a mysterious albino man mortally shoots Sauniere. The old, wounded curator holds together enough mental and physical strength to leave clues on the floor—but he was not leaving clues for the police investigators.

Sauniere has a family legacy; a centuries-old secret that has been passed down from the likes of Sir Isaac Newton, Victor Hugo, and Leonardo da Vinci. The secret was about to die with him. He had to leave clues for his granddaughter Sophie, a police code expert, so he arranged that she would meet a world famous Holy Grail expert named Robert Langdon. Together, they must discover the secret renowned artist Leonardo da Vinci left behind for the world to see in his famous painting of Jesus's final meal.

The boy pictures a scene from *The Passion of the Christ* where Jesus is holding the cup and telling his disciples to drink wine and eat bread to remember him. He vaguely remembers Bible verses he heard in Sunday school, where Jesus said:

Taking the cup and thanking God, he gave it to them: Drink this, all of you. This is my blood, God's new covenant poured out for many people for the forgiveness of sins. I'll not be drinking wine from cup again until that new day when I'll drink with you in the kingdom of my Father.

The boy shakes off these thoughts and goes back to reading *The Da Vinci Code*.

Sophie had lost her brother and her parents in a car accident. She was raised by her grandfather, who gave her puzzle codes to decipher for fun. Later, as a college student, she accidentally witnessed her grandfather taking part in a confusing secret ritual. Sophie and her grandfather hadn't spoken since. As an adult, Sophie began a career

GLOSSARY

Celtic: Referring to a form of Christianity that was practiced by much of the population of the British Isles from about the end of the fourth century until some time after the year 1171, when it gave way to the Roman Catholic Church's predominance; a modern-day renewed interest in this form of Christianity emphasizes God's love and inclusiveness toward all people; honor of Nature as God's "Second Book," and a feminist understanding of the importance of women.

consumerism: A prevailing preoccupation with buying tangible goods.

icons: Visual emblems that point toward meanings that are bigger than the visual image itself.

cracking codes for the Paris police department. Now, her grandfather's death brought her to the scene of the crime, where she found the da Vinci–related messages. Together, she and her new friend, Robert, would seek the truth of her family . . . as well as some surprising truths about the search for the Holy Grail.

The boy in the bookstore finally stops reading, walks to the cash register at the front of the bookstore, and buys the popular book. Like millions of other consumers around the world, his interest in religious ideas has influenced his decision to make a purchase. *The Da Vinci Code* is a bestseller that has made its author a millionaire.

RELIGION & MODERN CULTURE

The secular news media is important to Christian marketing these days. *Time* and *Newsweek* magazines have numerous articles about Jesus and Christianity. For example, in 2004, both asked, "Who killed Jesus?" At Christmas, they publish articles about the historical evidence surrounding the birth of Jesus. Journalists have also explored the topics of Christian popular music, the top evangelical leaders, and women in the Bible. Not only do these topics sell magazines—they also help stimulate religious sales in other marketplaces.

One reason Mel Gibson did so well in making a religious film is that he understands both media and religion. Gibson managed the media well in the debate about whether the film would encourage anti-Jewish sentiment and in the discussions about religious experience through violence. He was also wise to invite hundreds of the top religious thinkers in North America to watch an unfinished version of the film. He actually used the advice they gave, and they went back to their churches and colleges to tell everyone that it was a good film. This in turn brought thousands of viewers to his movie.

Religious people often look with dismay and disapproval at North America's *consumerism*—but the marketplace provides a great place for public debates. In North America, people vote with their dollars.

JESUS PRODUCTS

North Americans spend a lot of money on clothing and accessories each year. A popular bracelet among Christian young people in the past several years displays the letters WWJD (What would Jesus do?). It reminds young people (and some not so young) to ask themselves questions of behavior throughout the day.

"While church attendance may be declining, books and movies about Jesus are more popular than ever."

—*Robert L. Webb and Kathleen E. Corley,* Jesus and Mel Gibson: The Passion of the Christ

There is also a fashion Web site called WWJW: What would Jesus wear? Answer: Jesus T-shirts, of course. All over southern California, young people sport the T-shirt that reads, "Jesus surfs without a board." Pamela Anderson wears the "Jesus is my homeboy" shirt. These "homeboy" shirts are made by a company called Teenage Millionaire and sold on the Internet. Madonna has also been seen wearing a complimentary "Mary is my homegirl" shirt, according to Fox News Channel writer Catherine Donaldson-Evans. She quotes Teenage Millionaire partner Chris Hoy: "We looked at all the popular *icons* of the 20th century and Jesus definitely topped the list." Fox News reported other shirts as well: "My Savior is Tougher Than Nails" or "Go Fish" with the famous Christian fish on it. There are also belt buckles with the Ten Commandments on them. Such fashions have been available from Christian stores for a long time, but they have only recently been available in popular clothing shops like Urban Outfitters.

Cross necklaces and earrings have been popular jewelry items for Christians for a long time, but over the last twenty years, it has become a fashion item for people of all walks of life. Perhaps Madonna first made the big eye-catching cross famous in the 1980s. Now, diamond crosses, gold crosses, just about any kind of cross can be found dangling around the neck of almost anyone, anywhere.

Jesus tattoos are also seen everywhere with various cultural and religious implications. For example, Amaré Stoudemire, center for the

THE HOLY GRAIL: A POPULAR RELIGIOUS SYMBOL

The legend of the Holy Grail is a great place to understand the connection between Jesus and popular culture. The legend of the Holy Grail comes from popular traditions outside of the Bible. Some believe the cup—the Holy Grail—that Jesus drank from is magical, protected in some ancient vault. According to *The Da Vinci Code*, secret societies exist that have the explicit purpose of keeping the secrets of this grail. According to legends such as those described in the film *Raiders of the Lost Ark*, adventurers have been following clues and seeking this treasure for two thousand years. Through popular culture, we learn about these legends and traditions, including the stories in the Bible. For more information about the Holy Grail myths, you can read *The Grail, the Shroud, and Other Religious Relics: Secrets and Ancient Mysteries*, and for more on *The Da Vinci Code*, read *Lost Gospels and Hidden Codes: New Concepts of Scripture*—both in this series of Mason Crest books.

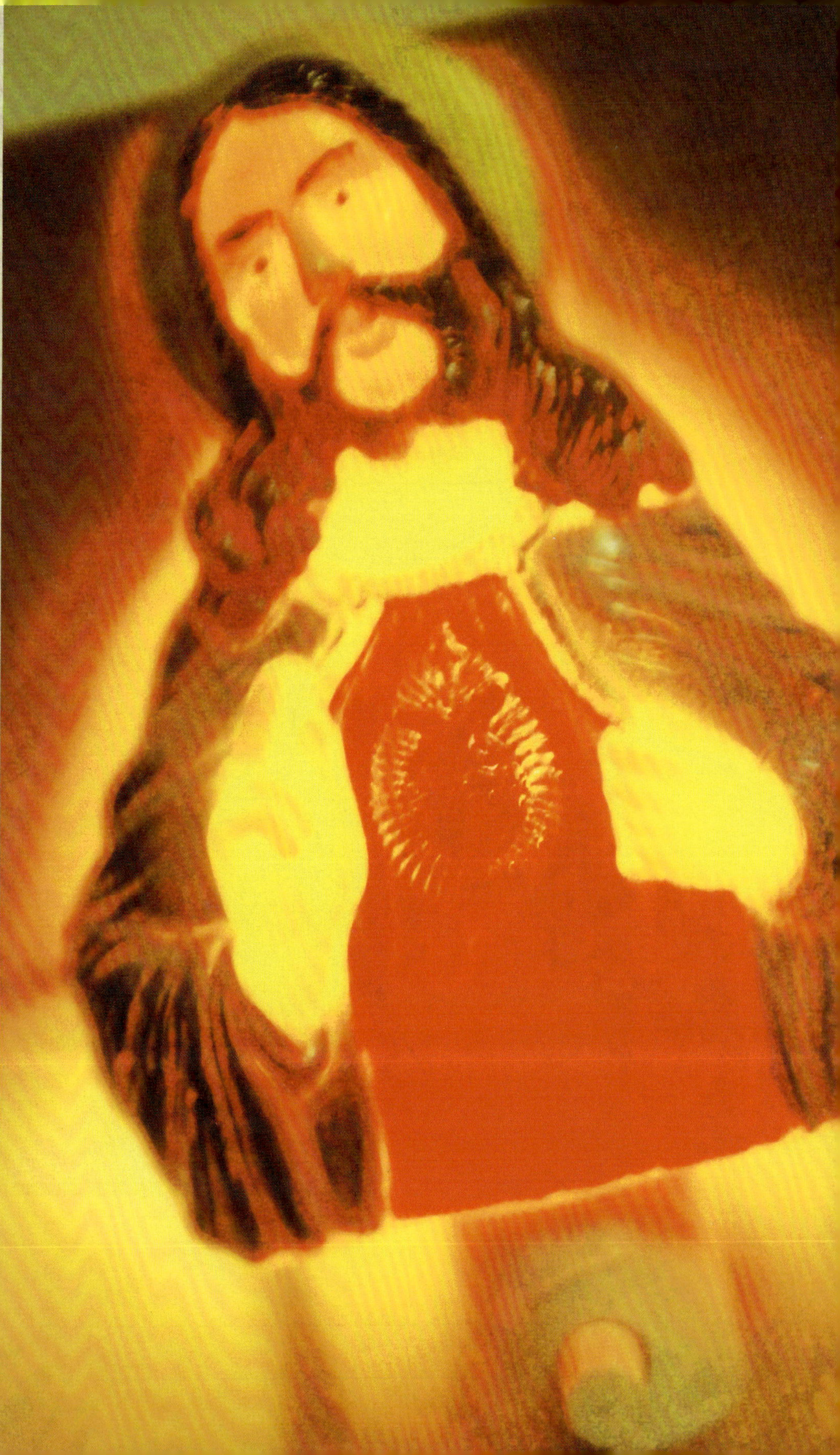

> *"Many contemporary Americans are shaped much more decisively by popular culture than by their formal education or their religious training."*
>
> —*Robert Jewett,* Saint Paul at the Movies

Phoenix Suns of the NBA, has the words "Black Jesus" tattooed in small script along the right side of his neck. This fashion trend leaves a permanent mark with everything from crosses to Mary. It is a lifetime decision to tattoo a picture of Jesus's suffering body on your arm or leg.

Less permanent statements are made by the famous Jesus night-lights, bobble-head dolls, and figurines like the one in the film *Dogma*. A company called Accoutrements makes these for Urban Outfitters, and Jesus dolls are catching on everywhere. In 2004, on MTV's show *Room Raiders*, a woman chose her date after she found a Bible on his dresser and a two-foot tall plastic lawn light of Jesus in the corner. Pointing at it, she said, "That's good because I'm down with the JC!" The guys in the van were happy about that; the inhabitant of the room was a Bible study leader.

It seems as though everyone in the contemporary world uses traditional Christian symbols. People with varied religious beliefs have adopted Roman Catholic rosaries, *Celtic* crosses and prayerbooks, candles with Jesus or Mary painted on the side, and various forms of the cross.

Some Christians are uncomfortable with Jesus's presence in the marketplace. Or if he is there, they think he should be pointing a finger of judgment—or leading believers away to a separate area filled with "safe," Christian versions of the products that fill the secular marketplace. They feel that using Jesus's image for financial profit is sacrilegious because they are using Christ for their own purposes—but they forget that Christian industries also make financial profits.

Canadian-born ABC news anchor Peter Jennings is known for reporting on biblical stories about Jesus. At the same time, he does not like to give his own personal religious views. In 2004, he devoted all three hours of prime time Monday to "Jesus and Paul: The World and the Witness." According to Jennings, the fact that it aired just before the release of *The Passion of the Christ* was only a coincidence. Still, he said, "In the wake of *The Passion,* which created such intensity, we bring some further education to the debate that people are having." Jennings' special was about St. Paul, who spread Jesus's message throughout the non-Jewish world after Jesus's death. Jennings walked through the present-day Middle East to learn the history first hand. He even showed how Jesus could have evaded capture by escaping into the desert.

Celtic spiritual leader George McLeod sees things differently. He states:

I simply argue that the Cross should be raised at the center of the marketplace as well as on the steeple of the church. I am recovering the claim that Jesus was not crucified in a cathedral between two candles; but on a cross between two thieves; on the towns' garbage heap; at a crossroad, so cosmopolitan they had to write his title in Hebrew and Latin and Greek . . . at the kind of place where cynics talk smut, and thieves curse, and soldiers gamble. Because that is where He died. And that is what He died about.

CCM CANADA

Christian record production is a profitable industry in the United States, but according to Anne Eapen, buyers in Canada have not responded to religious popular culture as much as their cousins to the south. At the same time, Canadians are buying more and more Christian music. Roy Salmond, who has produced many CDs during a career in Vancouver and Nashville, feels the industry is far more vibrant and healthy than ever before. Steve Nicolle, president of the largest distributor of Christian music in Canada, says, "The industry and music have never been better."

According the Gospel of John, Christ "became flesh and blood and moved into the neighborhood" (as translated by Eugene Peterson in *The Message*). In Jesus's day, the neighborhood was a rural, farming culture in first-century Palestine, where he used the language, signs, and symbols of the day to communicate the Gospel. Today's neighborhood is quite different, so the forms Jesus takes to communicate will also be different.

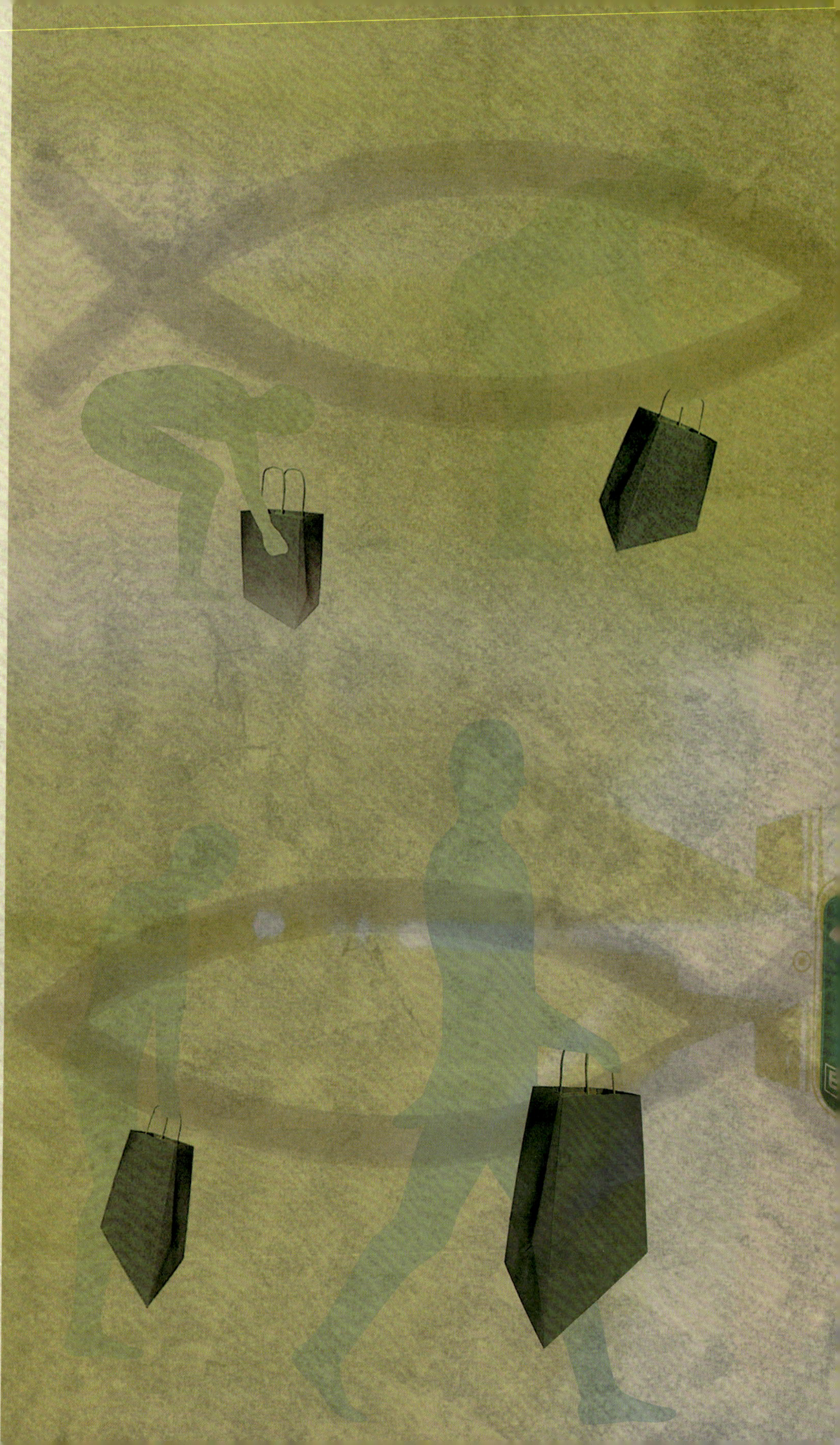

IDENTITY STATEMENTS

Many Christians buy identity products like a fish to put on the back of their car. Where did this come from? The ichthus (fish) symbol dates back almost two thousand years ago when Romans were persecuting and killing Christians. The letters in the Greek word for Jesus were similar to the letters in the word for fish. So, when two Christians secretly met, they would draw the sign of a fish on the ground to identify themselves, thereby avoiding detection by their oppressors.

From this perspective, the Passion and popular fads are not contradictory notions. Instead, it's only natural that Jesus should show up in the marketplace, where so many North Americans spend so much of their time. And in today's world, where so much of what we do revolves around the Internet, it would be surprising if Jesus didn't show up on the Web as well.

Chapter 6

RELIGION & MODERN CULTURE

RELIGION
ON THE INTERNET
Popular Culture's New World

A 2004 University of North Carolina study shows that teens claim to use the Internet for religious grouping more than for all other activities except for homework research. Forty percent of those teens who say that their faith is extremely important to them report using the Internet to visit religious Web sites a few times each month or more often. Clearly, the Internet has changed both religion and popular culture.

We are all swimming in a technological ocean, clicking our way through the waves. We surf from site to site, with no solid Internet land on the horizon. Even when we leave the keyboard, TV reality shows, professional sports, news magazines, hit films at the theater or on DVD, best-selling books, music, iPods, graphic advertisements, hip-hop videos, bloody computer games, and your favorite CDs are all part of this new sea of technology.

As fast as ocean waves come and go, they don't move and change at the speed of the wireless airwaves of popular culture. If an author were to write a story including the lyrics from current popular music, for example, those songs would probably be called "old school" by the time the book was finally published. No one knows what will be popular this time next year.

So what *is* this fast-moving flow called popular culture? Some would say that popular culture should be separate from formal religious culture, classical music, and high art. However, historical high art and classical music were the popular culture of their day, and when Shakespeare was writing plays, he was part of the innovative popular culture of his time. Now people consider his work "traditional" because it has been around a long time, but Shakespeare has never stopped being popular. Hollywood has produced several popular Shakespeare films in the past few years.

If we try to define popular culture, we would have to look at the fads shared by many people at any given time. Like the Internet, these fads connect us all in North America. Professors Craig Detweiler and Barry Taylor say popular culture relates to identity. It "both reflects who we are as people and also helps shape us as people."

Even when we are unaware of it, we often want to change our identity according to what is popular. For example, in school, students often talk about the most popular online computer games they played that day, share tips on what songs to download from Web sites, and buy clothes their favorite actors or rappers wear. Perhaps one reason these trends influence us is that people become popular when they reflect what is important to other people. Popular culture gives us a chance to ask, *What if* I was like this or like that?

Detweiler and Taylor also say popular culture helps unify people across North America and around the world. Think about this: at the same moment friends talk to each other about the reality show they all watched the night before, there are millions of other kids having the

GLOSSARY

blasphemous: Irreverent; treating something sacred with disrespect and contempt.

dualistic: Having to do with the theory that reality consists of two opposite elements or modes.

heretical: Departing from acceptable religious beliefs.

trinitarian: Having three aspects; each is often considered to proceed from the other rather than exist in any hierarchical relationship.

same conversation. People who play the same video games can talk in a shorthand that others cannot understand. When Snoop Dog added *-izzle*, to everything, we said *Sho' nuff*. The colored ribbons and rubber bracelets people wear tell others which good causes they support. We can understand our friends by the songs on their iPods. Popular culture provides many of the everyday languages we use to communicate in North America.

Jesus is definitely an important part of the popular culture, and contrary to what some Christians believe, "Many people have no issues with Jesus," writes Barry Taylor. "They are often more than a little interested, but they don't really know what to do about him." Jesus is just sort of there on television and in music, on T-shirts and in jewelry. Even nonreligious people respect Jesus these days, and people who connect to

RELIGION & MODERN CULTURE

JESUS IS MY SERVER

In 2000 in Brazil, Catholics decided to provide free Internet service as a way to connect with the people around them. Catolico, "the provider with a social mission," was offered to anyone, no matter their religion. No strings attached. The Associated Press reported, "Competition in the religious market is fierce in Brazil, the world's largest Roman Catholic country." The Catolico Web site was set up to allow people to get technical support, as well as to volunteer for community service or to give donations to orphanages. The Associated Press article quoted a priest: "Numerous companies also have approached the group wanting to place their ads close to images of Jesus." The priest added, "The Internet will not teach people to pray, will not raise their faith."

Jesus often do so more through popular culture than through organized religion. North Americans are not going to church as much as we used to, but we are often looking for spirituality, God, the truth, or simply the meaning of life's mysteries. Many say things like, "I'm not religious, but I'm spiritual." This is a change from the past.

"The Times They Are A-Changin'"

—*Bob Dylan, 1963*

"Things Have Changed"

—*Bob Dylan, 2003*

In spirituality, as well as in popular culture, especially on the Internet, information does not come down to us from the experts; it comes up from experience. Likewise, religious authorities from above no longer define Jesus. Nevertheless, at the same time, people are interested in hearing and learning what those leaders may say about God and spirituality, because spirituality in popular culture allows people to listen to a variety of ideas and then decide things for themselves. It allows people to ask good questions and explore their imaginations in ways that might be difficult to do in some religious settings.

The identity of Jesus has become more personal. In the past, if you wanted to know about Jesus, you might go to your priest or your pastor. These days, if you want to know about Jesus, you might first go to an Internet search engine.

SACRED VS. SECULAR: HAVE THINGS REALLY CHANGED?

Well, yes and no.

Bob Dylan first wrote a song telling the world that he thought everything was changing—then he went on to look back to see how much they had actually changed since 1963. Bob Dylan himself claimed to have converted to Christianity during that time, but he was not only talking about religion—he was talking about our culture, our world.

RELIGION & MODERN CULTURE

generation x

COUPLAND LABELS A GENERATION

Canadian writer Douglas Coupland wrote several best-selling fiction books in the 1990s about changes in culture. These books were popular with teenagers and young adults at that time. One of those books, *Generation X*, was the most popular. This title began to be used to describe an age group of people (maybe your parents) who felt that the world was changing fast. Another Coupland book called *Life After God* is about the experience of living in a scientific and rational world that had proven God didn't exist. The main character goes through life with no spiritual center. The surprise ending identifies a shift in North American culture where the main character wanted to find mystery and love—he wanted to find God again. This Canadian author put his finger on the pulse of a changing North American culture.

Over the past three or four hundred years, philosophy and religion tended to focus on an idea that religion and the rest of life should be kept separate. This idea has influenced political, financial, educational, religious, and other aspects of life all over North America and the Western world. The church was more responsible than the secular world for this

> *"Educated people are in no better position than the uneducated when it comes to knowing about God."*
>
> —*Fuller Seminary president Richard Mouw,* Consulting the Faithful

line of thinking. Following in the footsteps of ancient Greek and Roman thinking, traditional Christianity has tended to think of things in **dualistic** terms—black and white, good and evil, physical and spiritual—where one side of the duo is clearly superior to the other. (Celtic Christianity, however, provides a more inclusive and **trinitarian** alternative to this Greco-Roman concept.)

This has often created a shaky relationship between religion and popular culture. In church, this meant that one should avoid "evil" popular culture in favor of the "good" religious world. From this perspective, popular culture and religion are pitted against each other, so that "good versus evil" equals "religious versus secular." Some Christians would accuse popular culture of negative influences (promoting drug use, for example). Meanwhile, others have attempted to create a Christian parallel version to popular culture, trying to promote their religious messages through methods similar to the secular media. This is the route taken by Christian book publishers, as well as the Christian music industry.

The Internet, however, does not allow us to make these distinctions. There is no way we can draw a line across the Web and say, "This side is Christian and this side is secular." There may be Christian Web sites, of course, and other sites that are totally against Christianity—but both are equally available to users. The Internet is a good metaphor for modern culture, where the spiritual world and the secular world not only intersect; they are no longer always distinguishable one from the other.

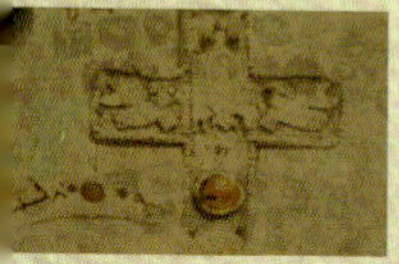

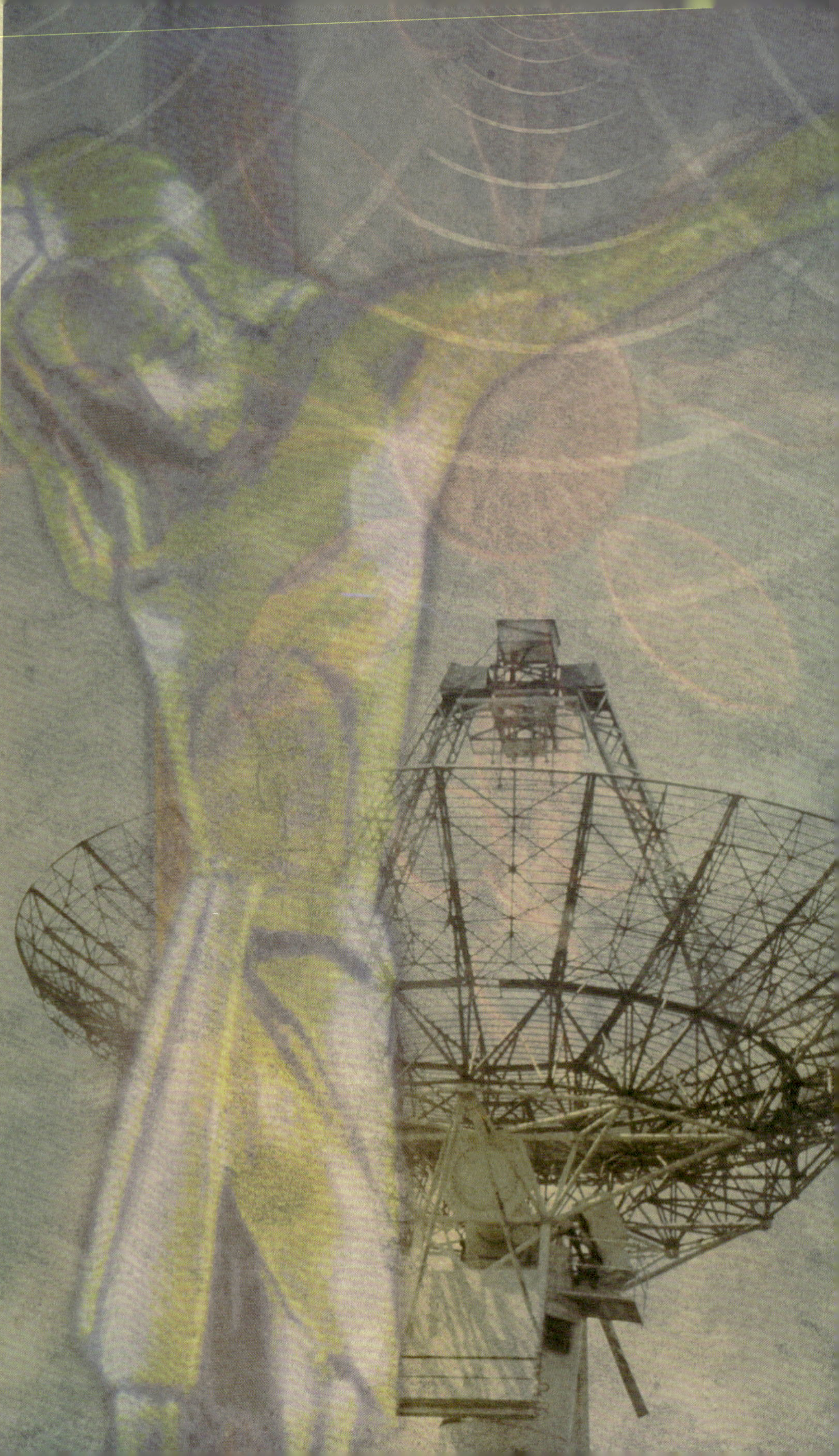

CANADIAN TELEVISION PROGRAMMING ASKS QUESTIONS ABOUT WHO JESUS REALLY WAS

In March 2005, both Canadian Learning Television (CLT) and The Biography Channel aired new Easter celebration programming. The CLT "History Monday" presented a special called *World in Celebration: Easter: The Jesus Mystery*. The online description read,

> As the furor surrounding Mel Gibson's *The Passion of the Christ* illustrates, the intense controversy and speculation that surround the story of Jesus' life and death rages on. With no body, bones, or even an identifiable gravesite left behind, only the testimony of eyewitnesses remains as evidence of this sacred event. The documentary *Easter: The Jesus Mystery* looks at how scholars are using ancient texts unearthed in Egypt to shed new light on this age-old story.

The Biography Channel's Monday programming competed with four weeks titled, *Paul the Apostle*, *Mary of Nazareth*, *Judas: Traitor or Friend*, and finally *Jesus*.

"Only an eternal story could shine through so many centuries of spin."

—*Telford Work, Westmont College professor*

Popular culture gives people a way to find all kinds of spiritual imagery, ideas, and traditions to follow. Many people today are not as interested in someone telling them all the right answers, as they are interested in learning more about the variety of possible answers in order to inform their religious choices. Media and fads have an important role in this.

Who was—or is—Jesus of Nazareth? Was he a divine visitor to earth as portrayed by works such as *Godspell* and *The Passion of the Christ*? Or was he the tortured figure caught between the conflicting demands of humanity and divinity in *The Last Temptation of Christ*? Is he a homeboy? A role model? A buddy? Was he even real? As people in modern culture interact with the story of Jesus, they grapple with the same questions: What was Jesus's mission and primary teaching? Was he human, divine, or both?

Some images of Jesus are held dear by many Christian believers and are considered to be the "true meaning" of Jesus. Other images were created to challenge or to attack traditional beliefs, and so have been considered by some Christians to be **heretical**, offensive, even **blasphemous**. Others see these less-traditional images as giving shape to culturally relevant questions, questions that can stimulate genuine spiritual reflection.

In the end, films, songs, Web sites, television shows, and products can all bring a new passion to our awareness of spiritual issues. They may in fact be perfectly legitimate ways to express spiritual experiences within everyday life. The world is full of mystery—and popular culture provides a forum where we can ask the questions that fascinate us all. *What if* Jesus loves these questions in popular culture?

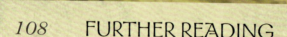

Barsotti, Catherine M., and Robert Johnston. *Finding God in the Movies: 33 Films of Reel Faith.* Grand Rapids, Mich.: Baker, 2004.

Brown, Dan. *The Da Vinci Code.* New York: Doubleday, 2003.

Burridge, Richard A. *Four Gospels, One Jesus?* Grand Rapids, Mich.: Eerdmans, 1994.

Corley, Kathleen E., and Robert L. Webb. *Jesus and Mel Gibson: The Passion of the Christ: The Film, the Gospels, and the Claims to History.* New York: Continuum, 2004.

Detweiler, Craig, and Barry Taylor. *A Matrix of Meanings: Finding God in Pop Culture.* Grand Rapids, Mich.: Baker, 2003.

Jewett, Robert. *Saint Paul at the Movies: The Apostle's Dialogue with American Culture.* Louisville, Ky.: Westminster John Knox, 1993.

Johnston, Robert K. *Useless Beauty: Ecclesiastes Through the Lens of Contemporary Film.* Grand Rapids, Mich.: Baker, 2004.

Joseph, Mark. *Faith, God, and Rock and Roll: From Bono to Jars of Clay: How People of Faith Are Transforming American Popular Music.* Grand Rapids, Mich.: Baker, 2003.

Marshall, Scott M., and Marcia Ford. *Restless Pilgrim: The Spiritual Journey of Bob Dylan.* Lake Mary, Fla.: Relevant Books, 2002.

Pinsky, Mark I. *The Gospel According to the Simpsons: The Spiritual Life of the World's Most Famous Animated Family.* Louisville, Ky.: Westminster John Knox, 2001.

Stockman, Steve. *Walk On: The Spiritual Journey of U2.* Lake Mary, Fla.: Relevant Books, 2003.

FOR MORE INFORMATION

CCM magazine Online
www.ccmcom.com

Hollywood Jesus,
Spiritual Film Reviews
www.hollywoodjesus.com

The Internet Movie Database
www.imdb.com

Next-Wave Church and Culture
www.the-next-wave.org

The Ooze: Conversations
for the Journey
www.theooze.com/main.cfm

Rock Rebel, Music news
with a spiritual twist
www.rockrebel.com

Rotten Tomatoes Film Reviews
www.rottentomatoes.com

Wanderings of a Postmodern
Pilgrim
pmpilgrim.blogspot.com

Yahoo Music
www.yahoomusic.com

Publisher's note:
The Web sites listed on this page were active at the time of publication.
The publisher is not responsible for Web sites that have changed their
addresses or discontinued operation since the date of publication. The
publisher will review and update the Web-site list upon each reprint.

PICTURE CREDITS

The illustrations in Religion and Modern Culture are photo montages made by Dianne Hodack. They are a combination of her original mixed-media paintings and collages, the photography of Benjamin Stewart, various historical public-domain artwork, and other royalty-free photography collections.

111

AUTHOR: Michael Evans is a writer who earned his master's degree in theology, focusing on Christian spirituality and popular culture at Fuller Theological Seminary. This is his first book, inspired by his teachers Barry Taylor and Robert K. Johnston. He works as a writing tutor in Pasadena, California. He would like to thank his teenaged students who read his first draft and gave him advice: Peter, Lisa, Nick, Todd, Allen, Michelle, Aaron, Karen, and Jeff.

CONSULTANT: Dr. Marcus J. Borg is the Hundere Distinguished Professor of Religion and Culture in the Philosophy Department at Oregon State University. Dr. Borg is past president of the Anglican Association of Biblical Scholars. Internationally known as a biblical and Jesus scholar, the *New York Times* called him "a leading figure among this generation of Jesus scholars." He is the author of twelve books, which have been translated into eight languages. Among them are *The Heart of Christianity: Rediscovering a Life of Faith* (2003) and *Meeting Jesus Again for the First Time* (1994), the best-selling book by a contemporary Jesus scholar.

CONSULTANT: Dr. Robert K. Johnston is Professor of Theology and Culture at Fuller Theological Seminary in Pasadena, California, having served previously as Provost of North Park University and as a faculty member of Western Kentucky University. The author or editor of thirteen books and twenty-five book chapters (including *The Christian at Play*, 1983; *The Variety of American Evangelicalism*, 1991; *Reel Spirituality: Theology and Film in Dialogue*, 2000; *Life Is Not Work/Work Is Not Life: Simple Reminders for Finding Balance in a 24/7 World*, 2000; *Finding God in the Movies: 33 Films of Reel Faith*, 2004; and *Useless Beauty: Ecclesiastes Through the Lens of Contemporary Film*, 2004), Johnston is the immediate past president of the American Theological Society, an ordained Protestant minister, and an avid bodysurfer.